T5-AOC-399

CHICAGO PUBLIC LIBRARY
HAROLD WASHINGTON LIBRARY CENTER

R0017199250

FORM 125 M

TL
.A1
D7
1973 Cop.1

**APPLIED SCIENCE & TECHNOLOGY DEPARTMENT**

The Chicago Public Library

Received OCT 14 1974

*The Book of
The Veteran Car*

*By the same author*
RALLY OF THE FORESTS

# The Book of The Veteran Car

Phil Drackett

PELHAM BOOKS

First published in Great Britain by PELHAM BOOKS LTD
52 Bedford Square, London WC1B 3EF
1973

© 1973 by Phil Drackett

All Rights Reserved. No part of this publication
may be reproduced, stored in a retrieval system,
or transmitted, in any form or by any means,
electronic, mechanical, photocopying, recording
or otherwise, without the prior permission
of the Copyright owner

ISBN 0 7207 0654 8

This book has been set in Garamond type, printed in Great Britain
on antique wove paper by The Anchor Press Ltd, and
bound by Wm. Brendon & Son Ltd, both of Tiptree, Essex

TO...
... all of us who have seen the dawn at
Hyde Park on a November Sunday morning;
... and to 'Beanball' whose 'medicines'
at Madeira Drive have often restored
life when it had been thought extinct.

## Contents

| | | |
|---|---|---|
| 1 | To Keep the Red Flag Flying | 13 |
| 2 | This was the Way it Happened... | 28 |
| 3 | 'The Brighton' | 40 |
| 4 | To Love and to Cherish | 51 |
| 5 | If you can't touch, just look | 63 |
| 6 | It isn't all gold that glitters | 80 |
| 7 | Stars on Sunday | 92 |
| 8 | Oh, for a Bottle of Gin... | 98 |
| 9 | Look Back in Affection | 104 |
| 10 | The Motor Car's Hall of Fame | 115 |
| | Index | 141 |

## Illustrations

*Between pages 48 and 49*

1. 'The world's first motor car'
2. Probably the first British four-wheeled petrol-engined car
3. & 4. Some of the evidence in favour of the Lambert being the first American motor car
5. Sir David Salomons demonstrating a Peugeot at the first motor show
6. The Hon. Evelyn Ellis in the Panhard which he and F. R. Simms introduced into Britain

*Between pages 80 and 81*

7. The 1898 Canstatt-Daimler
8. The front-engined Panhard which was produced in commercial quantities
9. S. F. Edge, with his wife and friend, aboard a Léon Bollée tricycle
10. The man who started Britain's motor industry, Harry J. Lawson
11. Herbert Austin at the tiller of the first four-wheeled Wolseley car manufactured
12. H. W. Egerton in his De Dion voiturette
13. Armand Peugeot brought his own Gallic flair to the new motor industry
14. The magnificent 1909 Rolls-Royce 'Silver Ghost'

## Illustrations

### Between pages 104 and 105

15  The 1913 Thames Coach
16  Early motor-cycles and cars on display in the Houthalen Museum at Limburg, Belgium
17  St. John C. Nixon, with co-driver Arthur Ayscough, and the Wolseley he drove around Britain in 1960 and 1970
18  A 1901 Mors heads the parade of veterans
19  HRH Prince Charles, with Lord Montagu, in the 1899 Daimler in which Edward VII took some of his earliest car rides
20  A selection of vehicles in the National Motor Museum
21  Kenneth More and Kay Kendall, complete with Spyker, in a scene from *Genevieve*
22  John Gregson in *Genevieve*

### Between pages 128 and 129

23  Designers of model cars work hard to be accurate these days
24  The 1904 Vauxhall alongside a modern Vauxhall Viva
25  Graham Hill takes the wheel of a 1903 Wolseley
26  The 1886 Hammel, believed to be the third oldest petrol-driven vehicle in the world
27  Denis Flather, in his 1897 Daimler, drives the Lord Mayor of Nottingham
28  One of the great racing cars of the pioneer days, the Rolland-Pilain
29  The author makes a presentation to Donald Healey
30  C. Chester Smith, of the Pembrokeshire Motor Museum, with a 1903 Oldsmobile

## Acknowledgements

The author's grateful thanks are due to the following for permission to produce their photographs in this book:
British Petroleum Co. Ltd. (BP): 1, 8, 13; RAC Archives: 2, 5, 6, 9, 10, 11, 12; Jack Lambert: 3, 4; National Motor Museum: 7, 14, 15, 19, 20; British Leyland Motor Corp.: 17; Fred Taylor: 18, 25, 28; J. Arthur Rank (Productions) Ltd.: 21, 22; Maurice Broomfield: 23; Autocar: 26; Ron Ockenden: 27; Western Morning News: 29; Western Mail: 30.

CHAPTER ONE

# To Keep the Red Flag Flying

The little old man spluttered in indignation. Behind him his veteran car spluttered in sympathy. Drackett, with his misplaced sense of humour, had just done it again and it looked as if for the first time that great and historic event, the RAC's Annual Commemoration Run for veteran cars, otherwise known as 'The Brighton Run', was going to feature a bout of fisticuffs as a grand finale to the day.

Fortunately for Drackett, the little old man—he looked as if he might have been useful with his hands in his day—contented himself with spluttering and he and his car chuntered away down Madeira Drive in keen competition with each other to see who could huff and puff the most.

What had happened? Well, it's a long story...

The year was 1956 and schemes were afoot to celebrate the Diamond Jubilee of the first ever Brighton Run in 1896. In charge of the RAC's plans for the occasion was Major Harry Stanley, at that time head of both the RAC's Competition and Press Departments.

My association with the Brighton Run only went back to the year before, so I was very much the new boy when Major Stanley convened a working-party to finalise arrangements. Bright idea No. 1 came up. 'We think it would be a good idea if someone dressed up in Victorian clothes and walked ahead of the first car at Brighton, carrying a red flag. We want a volunteer.' All eyes looked at 'junior'. Drackett was elected—with one disentient!

Bright idea No. 2 came up. A man I had always thought to be my friend suggested that it would be more dramatic if before Drackett led the procession he was first winched down on to Madeira Drive from a helicopter. 'Capital idea,' said the Major.

13

At this point, the newly-elected stunt man had to be forcibly prevented from leaving the room.

Fortunately, the Brighton authorities squashed idea No. 2 and refused permission for the helicopter to winch anyone down on to Madeira Drive. At least one coward was made a very happy man by this decision.

But the Major remained adamant about idea No. 1 and so the first Sunday in November found Drackett, outfitted by Bermans in deerstalker, knickerbockers and a Lord Kitchener moustache, carrying a red flag and marching down Madeira Drive at funereal pace ahead of a hundred or so veteran cars.

Halfway down the drive the procession halted and Drackett proceeded to hand out souvenirs of the occasion to all the drivers. Some of the old cars did not take kindly to the wait and when the little old man arrived for his souvenir, his car was boiling merrily and spouting clouds of steam. It was at this point that Drackett gave forth one of his utterances which a schoolmaster long ago assured him would one day get him hanged. He said, 'Put the kettle on and we'll all have a cup of tea.'

Let time cast a veil over the rest...

It was, of course, a silly remark. A remark made by someone new to this strange world of veteran cars, a remark which certainly would not have been made in after years when one realised just how seriously the enthusiast took this business of restoring, maintaining and running these grand old machines.

But, the uninitiated may ask, what is a veteran car and what started the veteran car movement?

The definition is fairly simple. In Britain at least, all cars built prior to December 31st, 1918, are veterans. Of these, those built prior to December 31st, 1904, are regarded as true veterans and are eligible to take part in the world-famous Brighton Run. The others are known as Edwardian veterans.

Cars built after this period but before the end of 1930 are vintage, a term often confused with veteran. A certain number of really good cars of the thirties are classed as post-vintage thoroughbreds and there is also a category of historic racing cars.

Some countries follow these lines of demarcation but not

## To Keep the Red Flag Flying

all. One large organisation in the United States, for example, labels all cars built before 1929 as antiques but divides them into classes according to age.

What started the veteran car movement is not so easy to pin down, although it is a not unreasonable premise that it all stems back to the Brighton Run. Certainly, the Veteran Car Club of Great Britain was formed as a result of one of these runs.

The man who started it all was Harry J. Lawson and it is arguable that history has been less than fair to him. He was one of the first men in Britain to see the possibilities of the motor car and to bring those possibilities before the public. It is true that he tried to make money out of his endeavours, the main thing his detractors have against him, but today in a world where 'business' and 'profit' are not necessarily dirty words Harry J. Lawson might well have had popular acclaim. Certainly he got things going—in more ways than one.

The late nineteenth century was ill-prepared for the arrival of the motor car. Roads were primitive, city streets were crowded with horse-drawn vehicles, petrol suppliers and garages were virtually non-existent. And magistrates and police, not to mention the great majority of the public, were very much against these new-fangled, smelly and noisy machines which, someone said, 'frighten the horses and put the coachmen off their beer.'

Some of the pioneer motorists fared better than others, of course. The Hon. C. S. Rolls, later of Rolls-Royce fame, used to recount the tale of how, when he brought a 3¾ horsepower Peugeot over from France, he obtained 'a kind of permission' from the Chief Constables of Hertfordshire and Cambridgeshire, whereby their policemen were instructed to look the other way when he came along.

One night he was going up the Great North Road when, about two in the morning, he came across a policeman on his beat. A friendly conversation followed with the result that the constable who, not surprisingly, had never been on a motor car before, begged a lift, saying that 'these 'ere things are so uncanny'. Once aboard, the man in blue urged Rolls to go as fast as he could—saying that he knew where the next man's beat began and it was safe to speed as far as there.

Rolls' experience was the exception, however. I recall the late Henry Mulliner who, at the time of his death, was the last surviving founder-member of the Royal Automobile Club, telling me of his conviction for driving a horseless carriage at little more than walking pace along Brighton sea-front. The RAC has in its possession two summonses issued against another pioneer, Walter Bersey, one of them alleging that he travelled at more than two miles per hour in Parliament Street. These were the last two summonses issued before 'Emancipation Day,' of which more anon.

Yet another of the RAC's early members, Frank Hedges Butler, later recalled, 'When we passed down lanes and along roads, the natives rushed to get behind hedges and into ditches, frightened at the wonderful and noisy machine and expecting to be run over.'

The laws governing such 'wonderful and noisy machines' were really tough ones.

Present-day motoring legislation began, to all intents and purposes, with the Highways Act, 1835. Until then, the obligation to repair roads fell upon the parishioners. 'Surveyors' were originally those responsible for seeing that work was undertaken and parishioners were compelled to give four days' labour a year, failure to do so resulting in a fine. Occupiers of land worth at least £50 per annum had to send a cart with its usual team of horses and two servants to work on the roads for six days a year.

As soon as vehicles came into the picture, even horse-drawn ones, more regulations were added to control them. Various Turnpike Acts were introduced, specifying the number of horses which might be used, this depending upon the width of the wheels. There were maximum weights laid down for specified wheel widths and if these were exceeded additional tolls had to be paid.

The Highways Act of 1835 did away with much of the earlier legislation, made the local authorities 'surveyors' for road maintenance purposes and for the first time created an offence of 'riding or driving furiously so as to endanger the life or limb of any person.'

About this time, steam-propelled vehicles were coming

## To Keep the Red Flag Flying

into use and various Locomotive Acts were passed to control them until the punitive Act of 1865 which, apart from its crushing effect on steam carriages, was later to inhibit the motor car. This Act laid down a speed limit of 4 mph (which could be reduced to 2 mph on the whim of local authorities) and insisted that a pedestrian carried a red flag in front of the vehicle. Much has been written about the red flag in relation to the motor car—what is not always realised is that this 1865 Act made the operation of steam-carriages impracticable for passenger-carrying purposes. It was back to horses or else transfer to the rapidly burgeoning railways. Had this Act not been passed, it is conceivable that steam-operated vehicles might still be running on our roads.

Incidentally, whilst on the subject of the law, present-day motorists might like to know that they do not have any modern Chancellors of the Exchequer to blame for having to pay vehicle duty. That ingenious stroke was introduced by the merry monarch, Charles II, as one of many measures to 'raise the wind', Charlie usually being in that sad state known as 'flat broke'. In 1790, there was an annual tax on four-wheeled carriages of £8. 16s. od. An Act of 1869 fixed the duty on carriages at rates varying from 15s. to 2 guineas and then in 1888 when mechanised carriages were referred to specifically, the sum was fixed at two guineas.

However, it was the speed limit imposed by the 1865 Act which most hindered the development of the horseless carriage. With France rapidly establishing herself as the leading automobile manufacturing nation in the world, it became obvious that Britain would fall far behind unless the law was changed.

Far-seeing men began lobbying, in Parliament and outside. It was a long job, demanding perseverance and patience but, eventually, in 1896, a new Locomotives on the Highways Act came into force. There was no mention of vehicles being preceded by a man on foot, with or without a red flag, and the speed limit was increased to fourteen miles per hour, although the Local Government Boards were still given the opportunity to reduce this to twelve miles per hour if they so wished.

Harry Lawson had been waiting for this moment. He had already formed the Motor Car Club and now he planned a 'Motor

Tour to Brighton' to celebrate 'Emancipation Day' and the freedom of the motorist.

Lawson was far from being a fool. He prophesied that special roads would have to be built to accommodate motor traffic, that the horse would become extinct as a means of transport, that war would be revolutionised by the aeroplane and that police would be equipped with high-speed motor-cycles. Now, as a preliminary to Emancipation Day and realising that the motor car was still on trial, he issued careful instructions to all those taking part.

'Motor Cars are on their trial in England,' the instructions read, 'and any rashness or carelessness might injure the industry in this country.' Drivers were accordingly urged to watch their speed and driving so as not to endanger other traffic and to treat police and other authorities along the route with polite consideration.

The warning as to speed flattered many of the cars intending to participate since they were not capable of approaching the new speed limit of fourteen miles per hour. But that it was very necessary to treat the police with kid-gloves was demonstrated by the experience of the three-car Bollée team which came over from France especially for the event. They arrived a few days beforehand and had to be towed from Victoria Station to their garage at the old Holborn skating rink by teams of horses, officious policemen reminding the drivers that the new Act was not yet in force.

Such pinpricks did not deter the jubilant pioneers who assembled with their cars in front of the Whitehall entrance of London's Metropole Hotel, shortly before nine on the morning of Emancipation Day, November 14th, 1896.

It was a typical grey November day, damp and misty with wisps of fog obscuring the scene and the Thames lying under a blanket of the evil-smelling stuff. Just the same, thousands attended the start, although some were late in arriving, their trains having been delayed by the fog.

A contemporary newspaper account (The *Daily News*, Monday, November 16th) said that 'it demanded the strategy of Napoleon, the daring of Nelson, the strength of Samson, the urbanity of a finished courtier, and the patience of Job, to force

## To Keep the Red Flag Flying

a passage across Northumberland Avenue from Charing Cross to Whitehall Place, where the merry motorists were bidden to breakfast.'

A dear old gentleman whom I knew well in the later years of his life, G. Shaw Scott, was twelve at the time and was taken to see the start by his father, a manufacturer of saddles and harness equipment. Mr. Scott Senior soon made up his mind: 'Noisy stinking things—they will never harm our business.'

His son, young though he was, thought differently and later became the first motoring correspondent of the *Birmingham Post*. 'But,' he told me, 'It took nearly forty years before I was able to persuade my father to buy his first motor car.'

After the cars had assembled, a distinguished gathering sat down for breakfast. It included the Duke of Saxe-Weimar and Jerome K. Jerome, the celebrated author. The tickets, incidentally, cost ten shillings 'inclusive of wine,' breathalysers not then being known, of course.

Bertram B. Van Praagh, one of the Vice-Presidents of the Club, made a brief speech on the objects of the run and then to the accompaniment of many a 'bravo', the Earl of Winchilsea tore up a red flag.

The Earl was to take part himself, accompanying the hero of the Paris–Marseilles motor race, Merkel, in a Panhard. The famous Gottlieb Daimler, who many believe to be the true father of the automobile, was there as a passenger with Freddie Simms, later to found the Royal Automobile Club, in a Canstatt-Daimler driven by Van Toll. Simms' friend, the Hon. Evelyn Ellis, was at the controls of his own Panhard-Daimler. The United States was represented by one of the earliest makes, the Duryea, of which there were two Motor Wagons taking part.

Then there were the Bollées, happily free of their horse-tows, and driven by Léon and Camille Bollée and their English agent, H. O. Duncan.

There were Panhards and Daimlers, a couple of electric cars and two Arnold Motor Carriages, derived from the Benz design, Walter Arnold being the English concessionaire of the German firm. One of these Arnolds was to be a regular entrant in the RAC Commemoration Run many years later.

Lawson himself and other members of the Motor Car Club

were resplendent in specially-designed uniforms which Camille Bollée laughingly said 'made them look like Swiss admirals' and someone else described as 'something between the garb of a yachtsman and the conductor of a Hungarian band.'

Yet it was strange and awe-inspiring to see these nineteenth century automobiles belching exhaust fumes and 'popping' incessantly as their owners made last-minute adjustments.

Daimler was presented to the Duke of Saxe-Weimar and then Lawson blew a warning-horn for engines to be started and burners lighted. Ten minutes to go.

All was bustle and flurry. The minutes slipped away rapidly, Lawson sounded the horn again and, amidst bangs and rattles, clouds of smoke and hiccuping splutters, the gallant cavalcade moved off.

Leading the procession was the car in which Emile Levassor had won the Paris–Bordeaux race the previous year. This Panhard now belonged to Lawson and, driven by Otto Mayer, it not only carried its new owner but also a purple and gold banner, emblazoned with gilt lettering.

Soon after the start, a number of cars were in trouble and unfortunately, as the official timekeeper had elected to travel in a Panhard which broke down several times, he was not at Brighton to check-in the first arrivals later in the day.

The cars went along the Embankment, over Westminster Bridge, past Kennington Oval and along the Brixton Road, doing their level best to stay bunched together. After leaving Brixton it was every man for himself and full speed ahead to the 'White Hart' at Reigate, where the drivers were to have lunch and obtain supplies of motor and lubricating oil. Agreement had also been reached with other public houses en route for supplies of water which many of the thirsty machines drank up in prodigious quantities.

Lunch was late that day for quite a lot of the participants. Breakdowns were frequent and some competitors had to tackle hills in reverse, not so much because the reverse gear was of a lower ratio than any of the forward gears but because the petrol ran more easily to the carburettor when the rear wheels were higher than the front.

There were two vans taking part, one of them driven by J. S.

## To Keep the Red Flag Flying

Critchley, works manager of the British Daimler firm. The other with Charles Rush at the controls, was the property of Peter Robinson's, the big London store, and was present primarily to act as a breakdown van, supplying mechanical first-aid to those who fell by the wayside. Alas and alack, the van itself kept breaking down and was soon trailing a long way behind the cars it was supposed to be helping.

There were many funny incidents and some where the humour was lost on those concerned. Duncan's Bollée crashed into a bank in trying to avoid a horse and cart which suddenly lurched into its path. Duncan's passenger was hurled out but escaped with nothing worse than mud-and-water stains on a brand-new suit. He gave up on the spot, thumbing a lift on another car. Duncan was made of sterner stuff and continued to work on the car in the hope that he might yet get to Brighton under his own power. But with night coming on he decided that discretion was the better part of valour and hired a horse and cart from a nearby farm to get him to the seaside town.

Unfortunately, his adventures were not yet over. Jolting along as fast as his four-legged 'engine' would go, he ran into some cattle in the darkness, killing a cow.

Others were having their troubles too. J. Russell Sharp was out of the run, his car having broken down completely, whilst the Earl of Winchilsea was not having an exactly trouble-free drive either. Nor was Henry Hewetson, the man who imported the first Benz car into Britain and who was riding that day in an Arnold Motor Carriage.

Indeed, only one man was bowling along to Brighton without a care in the world. He was the owner of one of the electric cars, a man who shall be nameless. He had driven straight from the start to the railway station where his machine had been put aboard a Brighton-bound train. It was unloaded at Preston Park, just outside Brighton, and the owner, an artist if there ever was one, proceeded to apply mud and dirt to the exterior of the vehicle to heighten the effect. Naturally, he was amongst the first arrivals in Brighton, as was another electric car, a fact which aroused the suspicions of those who pointed out that although arrangements had been made for fuel and water en route, nothing had been done about replenishing batteries and the electric car

*The Book of the Veteran Car*

had yet to be made which could cover the 50-odd miles from London without recharging its batteries.

During the run, the weather had steadily deteriorated. At Preston Park, another huge crowd had assembled under the dripping elms and weeping skies to welcome the survivors.

The Bollée three-wheelers of Léon and Camille were early on the scene, followed a couple of hours later by the Paris–Bordeaux Panhards of Mayade and Mayer, the latter, of course, with Lawson aboard.

Preceded by the Mayor and members of the Council the little procession chugged into Brighton in the teeth of a howling gale, led by the Presidential equipage and its banner with the strange device.

Those who arrived in time attended a Celebration Dinner at the Hotel Metropole, Brighton, which began at 7.30 pm. Exactly how many did get there was never certain, largely owing to the failure of the timekeeper to select a more reliable means of transport for himself. It is believed that fourteen cars completed the journey within the prescribed time but there is doubt as to whether or not they all covered the course under their own power.

The last-known arrival was the breakdown van which limped into Brighton at three o'clock on the Sunday morning.

Years afterwards, 'Monty' Grahame-White, like his more famous brother airman Claude, a pioneer motorist and a founder-member of the Royal Automobile Club, recalled the historic occasion thus:

'At the time I was 19 years of age, full of enthusiasm for all things mechanical and fortunate enough to make the acquaintance of Mr. Henry B. Merton, of 3, Palace House, Bayswater, a skilled engineer, through whose generosity I acquired a $\frac{3}{4}$ h.p. De Dion motor tricycle which he imported from France a few weeks before the London to Brighton run was heralded to take place.

'Henry Merton was the first Englishman to bring into England the framework of a Léon Bollée single-cylinder, air-cooled and tube ignition motor tandem, packed in sections and delivered by rail to London. For some months he had been experimenting in

## To Keep the Red Flag Flying

his private workshop with a system of electric ignition to replace the platinum tube and Bunsen burner, fitted to the two machines.

'For ten days before the start of the now historical Brighton Run, most of my road experience on the De Dion had been confined either to pedalling it with the back axle jacked up on a wood trestle or along short stretches of the Bayswater Road in vain attempts to get satisfactory results from the new system of ignition. As both machines had been entered for the coming event by Merton, he decided to refit the original burners and tubes to them. Two days before the event was to take place, I experienced my first satisfactory ride on the De Dion.

'Anxious to secure the best instruction available for the correct handling of the machine, I solicited the assistance of Charles Rush and Thomson Smith. They were considered, at the time, to be two of the most competent motor mechanics, and were in the employ of Harry J. Lawson at 40, Holborn Viaduct, the headquarters of the British Motor Co. Their services were rendered willingly. Others who profited similarly from their experience were one or two British pioneers whose names became famous in the motor industry in later years.

'Of the original 58 entries received by Harrington Moore, the honorary secretary of the Motor Car Club, 41 put in an appearance and 39 actually started. Some of their owners had to resort to hiring horses to set their vehicles in motion under their own power long after their official time had elapsed.

'Among those who experienced difficulty in starting their machines were No. 27, Merton's Bollée, No. 8, Gorton's Beeston (De Dion) tricycle, and No. 39, my own De Dion. They suffered from burner troubles due to water in the petrol.

'Whilst awaiting the arrival of new burner wicks and a supply of Carless Capel and Leonard's petrol, which I knew was reliable, I slipped into the Metropole for a cup of hot coffee. As I entered the now deserted breakfast room, I encountered a waiter collecting discarded menu cards and other decorations, such as miniature enamel badges of the Motor Car Club, and the symbolic Red Flag previously carried by a pedestrian in front of a mechanically-propelled vehicle when travelling on the highway; it had been ceremoniously torn in half by the Earl of Winchilsea

23

an hour or so earlier. Placing half a sovereign in the palm of his hand in exchange for this bundle of bunting I drank my coffee and have ever since retained in my motoring collection this historic flag. ['Monty' Grahame-White subsequently donated the remnants of the flag to the RAC.]

'The official order of procession was considerably deranged by spectators and temporary breakdowns soon after the start at 10.30 a.m.

'Within a few minutes of the arrival of the petrol I awaited, I set off on the first portion of the run to Reigate and had just reached the summit of Brixton Hill when the front wheel of the De Dion fouled the tram-lines outside the tramcar depot. The front forms and wheel were so badly buckled that all hope of effecting a repair to enable me to complete the journey to Brighton was out of the question.

'Entrusting my machine to the charge-hand at the depot I secured a cab and hastened to join Merton at Victoria for the special train to Brighton. Thus I had to content myself with seeing the arrival of the competing cars at the Metropole in Brighton instead of completing what I had hoped would prove a somewhat slow but successful run without serious mishap.

'A somewhat astonishing comment dealing with the official report of the result of this event, and the contradictory accounts of the performances of several cars which were officially stated to have completed the Run from London to Brighton without incident appeared in a French journal some weeks after its conclusion. Mystery surrounded the appearance of three or four vehicles outside the hotel in Brighton within a few minutes of the arrival of competitors who, along with many others, had neither seen nor encountered them after leaving the outskirts of the London suburbs. Included in their number were a Duryea, two electrically-operated vehicles and a Pennington tricycle.

'The early history of motoring is surrounded by controversy and speculation, with few alive today to challenge new speculations on what happened.'

Looking back at the hasty enthusiasm that organised so long a journey at such a time of year, at so early a stage in the motor car era, it seems remarkable not that so many broke down but that so large a proportion reached Brighton at all.

## To Keep the Red Flag Flying

The RAC records give the following as finishers:

|  | hr. | m. | s. |
|---|---|---|---|
| Lawson's Landau | 4 | 52 | 30 |
| Panhard et Levassor | 4 | 53 | 15 |
| Daimler Phaeton | 4 | 57 | 25 |
| Panhard et Levassor Wagonette | 5 | 7 | 13 |
| Daimler Dog-cart | 5 | 27 | 13 |
| Panhard et Levassor omnibus | 3 | 46 | 10 |
| Bersey Electric Landau | 5 | 4 | 40 |
| Bersey Electric Hansom | 5 | 41 | 30 |
| Britannia Electric Bathchair | 4 | 57 | 10 |
| Anglo-French Phaeton | 5 | 14 | 45 |
| Léon Bollée | 2 | 30 | 25 |
| Léon Bollée | 2 | 45 | 20 |
| Duryea Carriage | 5 | 2 | 0 |

This makes a total of thirteen finishers, but it seems fairly certain that at least one other, the Arnold which subsequently belonged to Edward de Colver, completed the Run successfully.

Undoubtedly, despite the failures, despite the weather, despite even the hinted-at sharp practice, the Emancipation Day Run did much to bring motoring to the attention of the British public and demonstrate the possibilities of the self-propelled vehicle as a means of transport.

Even more important, the Act which the Run celebrated was the first 'go ahead' signal, however limited, which the British pioneers of the automobile had received. Had it not been passed there might never have been a British motor car industry, an industry which today provides much of the life-blood of the nation's economy.

Emancipation Day is still celebrated annually—which brings us back to 1956 and those 'boiling kettle' Diamond Jubilee celebrations which began this chapter...

More than 200 cars manufactured prior to 1905 took part in those celebrations, amongst them one of the original Arnold dog-carts and an even older car from Spain. Crowds lining the route from Hyde Park to Madeira Drive, Brighton, were estimated as approaching two million.

Jackie Masters, co-founder of the Veteran Car Club, another who as a small boy had been taken by his father to see the

Lawson-promoted run, took part in the Jubilee event. So did J. Russell Sharp, only known survivor of the 1896 run, who went this time as a passenger in a car driven by the celebrated motoring historian, St. John Nixon.

And at the end of the Run, Wilfrid Andrews, Chairman of the RAC, stood up in his 1901 Benz and tore up a red flag, just as the Earl of Winchilsea had done sixty years before.

That red flag simply will not stay torn up, however. Today it remains a topic for controversy amongst motoring historians.

The Act of 1865 definitely insisted that vehicles should be preceded at a distance of 60 yards by a man carrying a red flag. The Emancipation Act of 1896 definitely contained no such provision. But in between came another act, the Highways and Locomotives Amendment Act of 1878. This made no reference to the red flag but stated: 'Secondly, one of such persons (i.e., the passengers in the car) while the locomotive is in motion, shall precede by at least 20 yards the locomotive on foot, and shall in case of need assist horses, and carriages drawn by horses, passing the same.' Thus there seems little doubt that although up to 1896, a man on foot still had to walk in front of the car, he did not necessarily have to carry a red flag.

My good friend, St. John Nixon, who died in his beloved Black Forest soon after emulating the great Thousand Miles Trial around Britain for the second time at the age of 84, used to get very hot under the collar about this red flag business and insist that those who talked about red flags after 1878 were wrong.

Legally, I think he was right. In practice, it seems that many motorists either were unaware that the red flag had 'disappeared' from the Act or thought it prudent, since they had to be preceded by a pedestrian anyway, that the man carry a red flag. Certainly contemporary accounts—and the speech made by Van Praagh in 1896—indicate that this was so.

Just as certainly, the reactions of magistrates varied from locality to locality. Perhaps some expected the red flag and others did not. When Winchilsea tore up the flag it was certainly a symbolic action but it seems hardly likely that this would have been done had the red flag really disappeared some 18 years before.

## To Keep the Red Flag Flying

In Valhalla, St. John is, I hope, arguing the point with Harry Lawson and Bertram Van Praagh...

Whatever the rights and wrongs of that argument, poor old Harry Lawson was 'Public Enemy No. 1' as far as the London police were concerned.

In the same issue of the *Daily News* which contained a report of the Brighton Run, appeared the following:

'At Bow Street Police Court on Saturday while Mr. Harry Lawson was taking his troublous way to Brighton, Inspector Pardo applied to Mr. Lushington for a summons against him. The Inspector explained that Mr. Lawson drove a motor car in the Lord Mayor's procession on November 9 in the Strand. The car passed through the City but the City police had taken no notice of it. The matter had been reported to the Commissioner in the usual course, and he had directed that a summons should be applied for against this gentleman for neglecting to have the car preceded by a man on foot. Mr. Lushington said that under the circumstances he did not think it worth while to grant a summons. The offence, if any, was a purely technical one.'

And so say all of us...

CHAPTER TWO

# This was the Way it Happened...

The Emancipation Day Run was the start of it all, but to the great mass of the British public the automobile was still an unknown factor, and so it was to remain for several years after that first journey to Brighton. The first moves towards bringing the automobile before a wider public came when Frederick Simms parted company from Harry Lawson and the Motor Car Club because he felt it was becoming 'too commercial'. Simms proceeded to found the Automobile Club of Great Britain and Ireland, later the RAC, Britain's oldest motoring club and the second oldest in the world, only the French pre-dating it.

This was to lead to Britain's first motor show, to the foundation of the Society of Motor Manufacturers and Traders, to professional driving instruction and many more developments which over the years have made the motor industry one of the most important cogs in the country's economical machine. Ironical in a way when one considers Simms and his reasons for leaving the Motor Car Club. But Simms himself was a keen businessman holding the Daimler rights in this country, co-patentee of the Bosch magneto and founder of Simms Motor Units, a thriving company which still exists today.

Yet the student of motoring history will tell you that the most significant development arising from the foundation of the Automobile Club was the great Thousand Miles Trial of 1900. This was the brain-child of that fabulous man, Alfred Harmsworth (later Lord Northcliffe) who was a member of the Club. And Harmsworth was ready 'to put his money where his mouth was'. He offered to indemnify the Club against any loss incurred in staging the trial—they had lost £1,600 in staging the Motor Show at Richmond the previous year—and also put up

## This was the Way it Happened...

£452 in prize money. Moreover, on the first morning of the trial, he proposed entertaining every competitor to breakfast at his country house near Theale, Berkshire.

This is to go ahead of the story, however. Harmsworth's idea was for a trial open to all classes of car covering a nationwide route and so bringing the possibilities of the horseless carriage before a wider audience than ever before. To further promote this aim, miniature motor shows and exhibitions would be held in the main towns and cities where the cavalcade stopped. The enthusiasts who then comprised the Automobile Club needed no urging and the energetic Secretary, Claude Johnson, was soon on his travels surveying a practicable route. Starting from London, he mapped out a course which took in Bristol, Birmingham, Manchester, Kendal, Carlisle, Edinburgh, Newcastle, Leeds, Sheffield, Nottingham and back to London, with exhibitions and hill-climbs at places en route, the towns and cities mentioned each marking the end of a day's stage.

The official programme of the trial is a massive tome which provides a unique picture of motoring in those pioneer days. The advertisements alone present an intriguing story. The Ocean Accident and Guarantee Corporation, assuring motorists that it had funds of more than a million pounds, proclaimed 'The Most Desirable Policy Ever Offered'. The Thornycroft Steam Wagon Company, whose vehicles were apparently used by Schweppes, claimed 'all the highest awards for steam vehicles on trial during 1899' and Coulthards of Preston, a rival firm, boasted that their steam vehicles were both oil and coke fired, coke being underlined.

To show that there is nothing new under the sun, a firm in Kettering was advertising strip maps in a case, the maps being turned so as to show the relevant section in a window on top of the case. This more than fifty years before Denis Jenkinson used a similar method to navigate Stirling Moss to victory in the Mille Miglia.

There was also an ad for 'The Motor Vehicle Users' Defence Association' an organisation in which the Hon. John Scott Montagu, Sir David Salomons, Frederick Simms, S. F. Edge and the Hon. C. S. Rolls were prominent. The object of the association was for the general protection of motor vehicle users against proceedings or actions at law, an objective subsequently taken over directly by the motoring organisations.

Amongst all the advertisements for motor manufacturers and traders was one from the Ariel Company promoting their Motor Tricycle and Whippet Detachable Trailer, 'the speediest, cheapest and most practical form of Motor for two persons'. The tricycle itself was a conventional enough motor tricycle but 'the Whippet was a pair of handlebars, frame and seat mounted on one rear wheel which attached to the rear of the tricycle. This contraption was capable of 35 mph. The illustration shows a typical lady of the period riding the Whippet with a gentleman up front. The mind boggles! It looks like an easy way to collect the insurance money on one's wife yet the makers say that the combination beat all comers in the road and hill-climbing contests held in connection with the Birmingham Motor Exhibition in January, 1900.

The Americans were already alert to the potentialities of the British market even at this period and the Locomobile Company from Broadway, New York, proclaimed the virtues of their steamer, 'free from noise, odor or jar.'

Even in those days, delivery dates were apparently a controversial subject and the Motor Manufacturing Company assured customers 'we shall not keep you waiting many weary months for delivery of your car and it is therefore in your interest to entrust your order to us.' MMC had no inhibitions either about what advertising agents call today 'knocking copy'. An ad for their motor tricycle includes this immortal paragraph: 'The engine fitted to this machine is made by the Motor Manufacturing Company. It has been considerably improved, is much more powerful, and less noisy than any French-made "De Dion" motor of the same type.' De Dion, on the other hand, claimed that their own cars were 'almost noiseless'.

Those enterprising motoring pioneers, Harvey du Cros and S. F. Edge, believed in their cars being all things to all men. The Napier Autocar, they boasted, was available with a 3 hp engine or a 16 hp one and could seat from two to sixteen persons. Again, the mind boggles!

But for one-upmanship, the palm goes to a firm called the Automobile Association Ltd., of Holland Park Avenue, who

*This was the Way It Happened* . . .

were selling a car called the Orient Express with the slogan 'Recommended for medical use'. Make of that what you will.

The Motor Carriage Supply Company was selling a tricycle under the name Simms Motor Wheel and this must have been one of the earliest attempts at a popular price vehicle, it being available at £115, a lot of money then but little in comparison with the £650 of the MMC 12 hp Phaeton, for example. The extraordinary Ariel Whippet was even cheaper, being available without the Whippet part for eighty guineas. Nor did you have to put all the money down at once for the Simms Motor Wheel, just a third with order and the balance on despatch.

Lanchesters wanted no gimmickry. As befitted a car which in many ways was ahead of its time, the Lanchester Motor Carriage was sold on its record—'The Highest Award For Perfection In Design' at the Automobile Club Show of 1899. This paragon of the virtues offered an 8 hp vibrationless balanced motor, safety tiller steering, electric magneto ignition, no batteries, range of speed at command and any speed up to 20 mph and carriage building and finish of the highest quality. What more could anyone want?

In contrast, Burford, Van Toll & Company, of Twickenham, offered the 'simplest and best two-seated car ever made.' So simple in fact that this was all they apparently thought necessary to place in an advertisement to sell their cars. No price, no details, just curt 'full particulars on application.'

The MMC Triumph was obviously aimed at a higher-class income bracket 'with a Dickey for Attendant'. That poor chap, apart from obviously having to push if the darn thing broke down, was perched precariously in what appears to be a baby's high chair slung behind the rear wheels. I wonder what he thought of the pleasures of motoring?

It says something for the motoring habits of the time that more than one advertiser, in giving the price of his wares, adds, as did the London Motor Van & Wagon Company, 'Hamper, one guinea extra.' And the choice of upholstery was between cloth or real leather. The same company also advertised the Parisien Touring Phaeton, with the extraordinary optional extra for £10 of a radiator.

The SS Motor Company—simple, silent, speedy, safe—were promoting a four-seater with accessibility to the working parts as a main sales feature. The body, it was said, could be removed merely by undoing six bolts.

Another company which obviously did not believe in any of this French nonsense was the Marshall Co. Their car, they said, was 'Made throughout in England. For use ON ENGLISH ROADS.' So take that all you Frogs. Despite this, Marshall's were not above also advertising The Renaux Motor Tricycle for which they held the English patents. This machine 'holds the hill-climbing record of the world' and in the Paris to St. Malo race, arrived first, having covered 226 miles in 7 hours, 11 minutes, at an average speed of 31¾ mph.

But Mr. Marshall, if such he was, could not subdue his patriotism for long. At the end of the advertisement for the Renaux, agreed in small print, was the line, 'Made throughout in England by the owners of the English and Colonial patents.' So remember your place, Frogs.

There was fighting talk from Roots & Venables, of Westminster Bridge Road, who claimed to be makers of the only safe petroleum motor car: 'This is the Only Motor Vehicle successfully using Petroleum OIL. Other Petroleum Carriages use Benzine, Petrol or Benzoline. Do not be misled by interested statements to the contrary, and rest assured Petroleum OIL has such overwhelming advantages over Petroleum SPIRIT for all Motor Vehicles that Spirit Vehicles are doomed to an early extinction.' The man who wrote that obviously missed his vocation and should have been a Prime Minister.

The Petrocar cost a modest £175 and, it was claimed, had run from London to Birmingham in the day on 2 gallons, 7 pints of oil, or a total cost of paraffin and lubricant of 1s. 6d. Tyres, however, were not so cheap. Clipper Pneumatic tyres cost £14 per pair for front and £25 per pair for rear wheels.

Hotels, on the other hand, seem to have been quite reasonable. A single bedroom at the Royal, Bristol, cost four shillings. The Bell at Gloucester would give you breakfast—tea, two eggs and bread-and-butter and attendance—for two shillings and the Midland at Birmingham offered dinner of soup, fish, joint or grill, sweets, cheese, bread and butter and coffee for half-a-crown.

*This was the Way it Happened* . . .

And if you did not mind a temperance hotel, Dear's at St. Albans would give you tea, bread and butter for ninepence. Petroleum spirit varied between 1s. 2d. and 2s. od. per gallon and competitors on the Trial were advised to order supplies from agents en route in advance of the start. Most of the agents were, naturally enough, motor traders, but some were chemists and it appears to be these gentlemen who sold the most expensive petrol although one of them did offer a reduced price for orders of two gallons or more.

In addition to the petrol agents, the organisers also arranged for a list of repairers en route to be available to competitors.

With all such details arranged, the Thousand Miles Trial needed only one more ingredient, entrants, and they were forthcoming in amazing quantity when one considers the year, 1900. In all there were 83 of them and on the great day, 65 actually started.

Amongst them were many famous names: E. M. Iliffe, later Lord Iliffe, the newspaper and magazine magnate; J. D. Siddeley, later Lord Kenilworth; Herbert Austin, later Lord Austin, the motor manufacturer; George and Frank Lanchester driving—what else—Lanchesters; and the famous racing motorist, S. F. Edge, in a car with which he is always associated, the Napier. Edge had with him a small boy, St. John Nixon, and thereby hangs a tale to be told later.

Before the start, there was a one-week exhibition of the cars at the Agricultural Hall, Islington, and at the conclusion of the Trial a similar exhibition at Crystal Palace. People were given rides in some of the cars, the proceeds going to the Mafeking Relief Fund.

So, on the chilly morn of Monday, April 23rd, 1900, the gallant 65 assembled at Grosvenor Gardens, Hyde Park Corner. The time was 6.30 am., and thirty minutes later the cars were flagged away on the first leg of 118 miles to Bristol. As might be expected, all sorts of mishaps occurred and the Simms Motor Wheel performed two complete somersaults, arriving at Bristol somewhat the worse for wear. These motoring pioneers were tough guys, however, and the driver of a 'works' Marshall refused to admit defeat when his water-pump broke. He carried on, filling up with water every five miles and eventually arrived in Bristol as midnight approached, having been 16½ hours on the road.

His effort paled by comparison with the feat (no pun intended) of 'Monty' Grahame-White, on the leg (again no pun intended) between Edinburgh and Newcastle. Making slow progress up a hill, Grahame-White decided to hand over the steering to his passenger whilst he exercised with a short run alongside the vehicle. The passenger promptly ran the car into a ditch, breaking the steering gear.

They were 52 miles from Newcastle, but the resourceful 'Monty' found that by standing on the step of the car, he could reach the nave of the front wheel on the driver's side with his foot and so control the direction of the car. And, believe it or not, in this fashion they continued the journey to Newcastle successfully—at the cost of a new pair of boots.

The most spectacular incident occurred on the Sheffield to Nottingham leg. Dudley Grierson, driving a De Dion, stopped in a hurry. The De Dion had a completely vertical steering column which meant that to apply full braking force the driver had literally to stand up, presumably the origin of the phrase 'stood on everything'. Mr. Grierson stood on everything. But he had badly under-estimated the braking power of his car and—whoosh—he was thrown right over the wheel and over the front of the car. The car then rolled forward over him, fortunately without damaging him. Could this be the earliest recorded argument for fitting seat-belts?

The youthful Nixon recalled: 'Some indication of traffic conditions will be gathered when it is recorded that for the first 4½ miles to Hammersmith, the maximum speed permitted by the Club regulations was 8 mph, but this was reduced still further to 6 mph through Maidenhead. There was a toll-gate just beyond Maidenhead Bridge which entailed the toll of 2d. per wheel and no car was allowed to take less than 14 minutes through Maidenhead.

'Charlie Friswell broke the starting-handle on his rear-engined Peugeot and fearful lest he might not be able to get a "push" start, he decided to keep the engine running the whole day, including stops for meals, etc. A Lanchester car broke its valve-gear bracket and had to be pushed several miles. An almost

*This was the Way it Happened* ...

constant flow of new parts was required by an MMC motor tricycle. At the end of the Trial, it was jokingly said that the only part of the original machine was the switch.

'At the end of the Trial, to assist further the Transvaal War Fund, runs were given on some of the faster cars for 2s. 6d. per passenger.'

Thirty-five of the original 65 completed the course.

The manufacturers' awards went to Benz, Wolseley, Daimler and Ariel for winning their classes, although there were no awards for cars selling at more than £500, motor-cycles carrying one person only and public service vehicles.

The only Gold Medal of the Trial for the vehicle which 'is the most meritorious irrespective of class, the owner having accompanied the vehicle throughout and having driven and steered at least half the distance', was awarded to the 12 horse-power Panhard, owned and driven by the Hon. C. S. Rolls, and reputedly the fastest car in Britain at the time.

Ten cars were awarded Silver Medals, amongst them the only woman driver in the event, Mrs. Bazalgette's Benz Ideal. Four others were awarded Bronze Medals including a Daimler, driven driven by H. R. Langrishe but owned by Alfred Harmsworth, the man whose idea it all was.

It had been a tremendous success with large crowds everywhere, headed in most cases by the senior citizens of the locality. The British public had become aware, as never before of the existence of the motor car.

In 1903, another Thousand Miles Trial was organised. Many new tests were included, braking and 'dust raising' amongst them, and the road section consisted of a series of separate routes, all starting from the Crystal Palace and journeying to and from Margate, Folkestone, Bexhill, Eastbourne, Brighton, Worthing, Southsea and Winchester. In 1908, this was followed by an even more ambitious Two Thousand Miles Trial. Both events were highly successful, but modern historians are emphatic that the Trial of 1900 represented the big breakthrough for the motor car in this country.

It was to be commemorated sixty years later when St. John Nixon, one of the survivors of the 1900 event, and Arthur Ayscough, followed the original route in the only surviving car, an 1899 Wolseley, which afterwards went on display at the RAC.

Nixon was 14 when he took part in the original trial and 74 when he re-enacted it. Ten years later he was to do it again to celebrated the 70th Anniversary of the Trial, a remarkable achievement for a man of his age.

This anniversary was also commemorated by the Veteran Car Club with a 'round Britain' trial culminating in a banquet in the City.

It must not be imagined that great motoring events were at this time confined to the United Kingdom. Apart from the great Continental point-to-point motor races, there were epics such as the Peking to Paris event, sponsored by the French newspaper, *Le Matin*. It was not a race in the usual sense but rather a test of endurance and the newspaper said that all competitors who covered the ten thousand mile journey successfully would be deemed to have put up performances of equal merit.

It was a great idea but even the hardy pioneers of the early 1900's thought twice about a journey in which one would almost certainly encounter snow, sand and Chinese warlords. Thus, when the big adventure began on June 10th, 1907, only five cars set off from the winding streets of the capital of the Celestial Empire, under the slant-eyed gaze of inscrutable Orientals and budding Fu Manchus.

There were two De Dions, driven by Cormier and Collignon, entered by the works; Prince Scipione Borghese in his own giant Itala; and two more 'works' cars, a Spyker, with Goddard at the wheel; and the spidery little Contal tricar, whose driver, Pons, must have been a brave man indeed.

A long line of coolies trudged beside the cars as they headed for Nankow, a precaution which soon proved its worth. The rains came earlier than expected and the coolies were soon hard at work digging the cars out of the mud. Conditions were bad enough for the strong and sturdy Itala but for the little Contal they were well-nigh impossible. The coolies gave up and returned to Pekin and Pons decided to follow their example. Reaching a railway line, he had the Contal sent ahead by train.

It had been the intention of the five to stick together but the inability of the Contal to keep up had destroyed that plan and

## This was the Way it Happened...

the Itala, going well, now proceeded to put distance between itself and the other survivors.

Their adventures as they followed the Great Wall of China, crossed the Gobi Desert and battled through Siberia, would, —and have—filled a book. By the time they reached Moscow, the Italians were heroes and the rest of their journey to Paris was one, long triumphal procession. Two months after leaving Pekin, Borghese and his co-drivers, Barzini and Giuzzardi, drove into Paris to a wonderful welcome, a welcome which was almost matched a couple of weeks later when the two Frenchmen, Cormier and Collignon, also arrived.

The following year, a 'Round The World' race from New York to Paris was staged. It was won by the American Thomas Flyer but again, Itala cars distinguished themselves.

Then, in 1909, the Guggenheim Trophy was held, the winner being the first car to blaze the trail across America from New York to Puget Sound, a distance of some 4,000 miles. This, too, attracted a five-car entry. Henry Ford, striving to establish himself as a major motor manufacturer, entered two Model T's, one to be driven by Frank Kulick, who had been winning race after race for Ford, and H. B. Harper, the other by Bert Scott and C. J. Smith.

Lined-up against them were an Itala, a Shawmut and an Acme.

The start, on June 1st, 1909, was from City Hall in New York and was honoured by the presence of President Taft.

The crews found it pretty much plain sailing as far as St. Louis but after that the rain and the floods came and they had to make frequent detours. The ultra-light Fords were easier to handle in the conditions than their heavier adversaries and the Ford drivers also blessed the chain of Ford dealers dotted strategically across the continent. These agents had been warned to look out for the two Fords and to give every assistance. Interesting to note that some sixty years later, the same sort of system gave Fords victory in the London to Mexico World Cup Rally, the East African Safari and the RAC International Rally of Great Britain.

Race reports appearing in the American press were alarming. So much so that when the crew of the Itala struggled into Cheyenne they found a wire from the owner of their car ordering them to abandon the race and ship the car to Seattle by train.

The remaining four cars battled on through Wyoming, Idaho and Oregon into the state of Washington, the finish now close at hand. One barrier remained—the Cascade Mountains and, although the month of June was well-advanced, deep snow lay in the pass through the mountains.

Scott and Smith were leading in Ford No. 2 when Henry Ford, impatiently awaiting their arrival in Seattle, had a great idea. He hired a gang of labourers and went up into the mountains from the western side. They linked with the leading car and went ahead of it, digging a trail through the snow. Behind them, Ford No. 1 was in trouble, having hit a snow-concealed rock. Harper and Kulick, alone as they were, had to set to and repair it.

Meanwhile Ford's enterprise had paid off and Scott's car drove into Seattle to a tumultuous welcome from 80,000 spectators. It had covered 4,106 miles in 22 days, 55 minutes, and when it reached Seattle it still had good New York air in at least two of its tyres.

At the banquet to honour the winners, Robert Guggenheim handed over the trophy with the comment, 'Mr. Ford's theory that a lightweight car, highly powered for its weight, can go places where heavier cars cannot go and can beat heavier cars costing five or six times as much on the steep hills or on bad roads, has been proved. I believe Mr. Ford has the solution of the problem of the popular automobile.' He was right. By the time, production ceased in 1927, the Model T had sold 15 million.

Only one of these great early events mentioned, the Brighton Run, has since been commemorated with regularity. But there is one another—the Glidden Tour, which might be described as America's equivalent of the Commemoration Run, although its usual route, New York to Detroit, is one thousand miles compared with London to Brighton's fifty-three.

The first Glidden Tour was organised by the American Automobile Association in 1905. The objectives were very similar to those of our own Automobile Club in running the Thousand Miles Trial: to demonstrate to a sceptical public that the motor

*This was the Way it Happened* ...

car had come to stay and was just as reliable a means of transport as a horse and buggy.

The Glidden Tours were organised every year until 1913 but then lapsed until revived after the Second World War by the Veteran Motor Club of America. Subsequently, the tour was organised in alternate years by the Veteran Motor Club and the Antique Automobile Club. A third body, the Horseless Carriage Club, separated by more than 3,000 miles from the two Eastern-based clubs, launched its own National Western Tour.

In such ways is the spirit of the pioneers recaptured and remembered.

CHAPTER THREE

## *'The Brighton'*

Let pedants and historians argue about the comparative merits of the original Emancipation Day Run and the great Thousand Miles Trial. The fact remains that Emancipation Day is still commemorated annually in an event organised by the Royal Automobile Club on the first Sunday of November, an event which attracts entries from all over the world and hosts of spectators, numbered conservatively by the hundreds of thousands.

Who first thought of commemorating the anniversary of Emancipation Day, no one now remembers. It was presumably a member of the infant Automobile Club of Great Britain and Ireland (now the RAC), since that Club organised the first few celebrations in the years immediately following Emancipation Day. But they bore little resemblance to the Run of today and were more in the nature of tours for members. Indeed, some of them did not have Brighton as their final destination so the link with Emancipation Day was a flimsy one.

The true forerunners of the London to Brighton came in the 1920's when *The Autocar* magazine persuaded the *Daily Sketch* and the *Sunday Graphic* to promote what they called 'The Old Crocks' Run to Brighton', a name which clung to the event for many years, is hated by all participants and can still earn a punch on the nose for the layman careless enough to use it in the presence of a dyed-in-the-wool veteran car man.

These runs were 'conducted by the Royal Automobile Club', the programme was free—and perpetuated the legend about the the man with a red flag, there was a gold medal for the most meritorious performance and the finish was at Patcham, the cars afterwards parading through Brighton.

Forty-four cars took part in the 1928 Run, of which the oldest were two Panhards, one dated 1891 and the other 1893.

40

## 'The Brighton'

There was an original Thornycroft steam wagon and the youngest cars taking part were of 1903 vintage. One of these, an Oldsmobile, had been found on a dump in Manchester and purchased for the magnificent sum of £5.

Run by the newspapers as a promotional gimmick, the London to Brighton speedily caught the public imagination, and it became obvious that it was worth continuing as a serious motoring event. So, in 1930, with the consent of all parties, the RAC took over the sole responsibility of organising the event and it has been held annually ever since with, of course, the exception of the war years.

From the start of the RAC's reign, it was decided that there should be no awards of a competitive nature but that all those finishing the course within a certain time limit should receive an award, initially certificates and later commemorative plaques.

There were 58 entries for the first Run under the new regime ranging from Jimmy Allday's 1894 Benz to C. Dugdale's 1904 Renault.

Sammy Davis's Léon Bollée, found in a French farmyard and purchased for a handful of francs, was in the lists. So too was R. O. Shuttleworth's 1897 Panhard, originally owned by Lord Rothschild and fourth in the 1898 Paris to Amsterdam race. E. G. Blake's 1897 Benz stood in a field for years. A tree grew through the back and had to be chopped down before the car could be moved. Another car which had had its troubles was the unusual 1898 Vipen, said to have been buried at the foot of Hindhead for 22 years.

This 1930 Run also saw the appearance of the Stephens, driven by the son of its builder, which was to be a regular in the event for many, many years. There was too, an 1898 Star, one of the first ten cars built by the Star Motor Company, which had taken part in the Thousand Miles Trial and earned an award.

Not to be outdone by the Benz and the Vipen, three other owners claimed that their cars had been used as hen roosts, one said his had been in a shed for fifteen years and another in a field for a like time. R. G. Davies went one better, saying that his De Dion Bouton had been used as a dog kennel.

A sounder historical background belonged to the 1903 Siddeley, entered and driven by J. D. Siddeley, CBE, which was the first car to be driven on Brooklands race track.

But one entrant gave pride of place to no one. D. M. Copley was so proud of his 1898 Daimler that he challenged any other old car to a 200-mile race. The challenge does not appear to have been accepted.

The competitive spirit appears to have been too prevalent amongst entrants for in 1931 the organisers deemed it prudent to put a pilot car in the lead 'to prevent competitors attempting to race.' Presumably, much to the disgust of Mr. Copley.

There were 57 entries this time, the oldest being Jimmy Allday's 1894 Benz, believed at that time to be the oldest car in the country in running order. Edward de Colver's 1896 Benz (afterwards more correctly described as an Arnold) made the first of its many Commemoration Runs, having taken part in the original Run in 1896. The most unusual vehicle in the event was an 1898 Chas. T. Crowden, with a petrol engine that followed steam practice. In contrast, a 1903 Mercedes was said to be capable of over 80 mph in racing trim.

'Not just a pretty face' was W. Keppel's 1901 De Dion Bouton which was used for many years by the *Eastern Daily Press* to carry newspapers from Norwich to King's Lynn.

Although the early thirties were bleak years for many with the Wall Street crash, unemployment and hunger marches very much lingering in the air, the Brighton Run continued to grow in popularity and the entries increased steadily. In 1932 there were 72, by 1938 there were 121.

Many well-known drivers made their appearance in the Run, amongst them the Singer rally expert, Stanley Barnes, one-time Competitions Manager of the RAC; world record-breaker Sir Malcolm Campbell, who drove a 1904 Sunbeam; the motoring historian Kent Karslake and the author of many books on the steam railway and veteran cars, L. T. C. Rolt; pioneer George Lanchester; racing motorists A. Powys-Lybbe and the Hon. Brian Lewis, later Lord Essendon; and Fred Bennett, whose exploits with Cadillac had long ago won him the RAC's coveted Dewar Trophy.

The programme was no longer free (it cost 3d.) and each car in the Run was insured by the organisers for £100, a goodly

'The Brighton'

sum considering that a 1901 Wolseley entered in the 1934 Run had been purchased by Mrs. Shuttleworth for fifteen shillings.

There were almost more racing drivers in the Brighton Run than on the race circuits. 'B. Bira', the Siamese ace, appeared in a 1903 Oldsmobile in 1935 and in a 1902 Peugeot the following year; Philip Fotheringham-Parker turned up on an 1899 Century Tri-car in 1936; and Tommy Wisdom in 1938 drove a 1900 Wolseley which won an award in the Thousand Miles Trial, the Silver Medal of the Automobile Club of France and the *Daily Mail* prize. But probably the most interesting car around this time was a 1904 Lagonda Tri-car fitted with frontwheel brakes besides one on the back wheel and known as 'the motor-cyclist's Mercedes'.

Although the Run was going from strength to strength, war clouds were looming over Europe and by the time the first Sunday in November, 1939, came round, the nation was at war.

It was seven years, before the veterans would once again set off on the road to Brighton . . .

When the Run recommenced in 1946, there was a surprisingly good entry considering all that had happened in the long years between. It seems reasonable to assume that with owners away and some, alas, not returning, cars were often neglected and, since the Home Front was under constant attack, it would be astonishing if every veteran car in the country escaped unscathed by the bombs. Yet, despite this, no less than 137 cars lined up for the resumption. The oldest was one of the 1896 Léon Bollées, the youngest a 1904 Humber. The drivers included Stanley Barnes, Sammy Davis, St. John Nixon, Philip Fotheringham-Parker, Norman Reeves, Tommy Wisdom, Sir Clive Edwards, Stanley Sears, D. C. Field (the historian whose 'Notes on the Cars' still appear in the programme, revised each year, to this day), F. W. Hutton-Stott, C. W. P. Hampton, T. W. Lightfoot, Jack Kemsley, Alan Hess, Richard Dimbleby (the illustrious BBC commentator), Fred Bennett, John Bolster, Victor Riley and Jackie Masters. Most of these drivers were to be familiar figures on the Brighton Run for many a year to come.

And, appropriately enough, one of the 137 entries, a 1900 Peugeot, appeared in a film entitled, *Those Were The Days.*

A similar field took to the A23 the following November but in these early post-war years there was as yet no sign of the boom to come.

By 1948, the entry had dropped to 120 with the oldest car, Sammy Davis's 1897 Léon Bollée and the youngest a 1904 De Dion Bouton, unearthed on the Isle of Sheppey back in 1931. A more recent discovery was a Baby Peugeot, owned by Dr. W. A. Taylor, which had come to light after the 1946 Run, being discovered in an ironmonger's shop.

Another Baby Peugeot sounded more like a horse from the description given: delivered from Paris works in February, 1903, but given away in 1904 as 'uncontrollable'. Uncontrollable or not, the little car was to complete successfully a number of Brighton runs.

Within a year or two, the downward slide had been halted and the number of entries began to increase. There were 163 in 1950, 166 in 1951 and 163 again in 1952.

Well-known names continued to add lustre to the event. In 1952 a youthful Stirling Moss appeared as co-driver to Fred Bennett in the latter's Cadillac, and another passenger was the famous rally driver and Monte Carlo Rally winner, Maurice Gatsonides.

Percy Kidner, pioneer Vauxhall driver, record-breaker and engineer, drove the 1904 Vauxhall which, a few years later appeared in a commercial television programme with the lovely Muriel Young as passenger and myself as 'driver'. The quotes are because either Vauxhall or the TV producer, and I cannot remember which, did not trust me to drive the car in the studio (and I do not blame them) so the motive power was provided by three or four sweating stage-hands. Surely the quietest running veteran car of all time.

The upward trend continued in 1953 when there were 181 entries and by now international interest was being aroused. In 1954, the Danish Automobile Club entered the oldest car yet seen in the event, an 1886 Hammel, which was allowed to start thirty minutes ahead of the others so as to give it unimpeded passage. The total entry soared to 223 and amongst the 'pilots' was racing-driver Ken Wharton in a 1901 Albion and speedway ace Oliver Langton in a 1904 Rolls-Royce.

## 'The Brighton'

1955 provided a double celebration. It was the Silver Jubilee Year of the Veteran Car Club and it also marked the 25th Anniversary of the RAC's 'take-over' of the Run. There were again over 200 entries, 213 to be precise, ranging from Edward de Colver's 1896 Arnold, to H. Trussell's 1904 Reo.

A contrast between ancient and modern was provided by the RAC's Aerial Patrol, a Westland Dragonfly Helicopter being used for air-to-ground traffic and liaison purposes. Crowds were getting bigger and bigger and the RAC and the police found it advisable to signpost two alternative routes to Brighton for those who wished to make sure of getting to the seaside in time for the finish.

1956 was another celebration year, the 60th Anniversary of the original event, some aspects of which we touched upon in Chapter One. A record entry of 231 cars marked the occasion, No. 1, an 1895 Panhard-Levassor, coming from Spain, the first-ever Spanish entry. Notable drivers included the father-and-son racing team of Lewis and Stuart Lewis-Evans; cartoonist Russell Brockbank; Richard Dimbleby; Lord Montagu; Charles Chester Smith, whose Pembroke museum later became a great attraction to veteran car enthusiasts; C. F. Caunter, Curator of the transport exhibits at the Science Museum and the speedway brothers, Oliver and Eric Langton.

Traditionally, cars were greeted on arrival at Brighton by the incumbent Mayor but on this occasion, Mr. Mayor, in the person of Councillor C. Cohen, accompanied Norman Reeves in his 1904 Darracq.

Caunter was back the following year with a very old car indeed—an 1888 Roger Benz. Like the Hammel three years previously the Roger Benz was permitted to start half an hour in advance of the other entrants, in view of the age and the very low maximum speed this historic machine was capable of maintaining. The car was also to take part the following year but met with a calamity when a thoughtless driver of a modern vehicle baulked it and the Roger Benz's brakes were not equal to the task.

Entries remained high—236 in 1957. There was a slight drop to 205 the following year but for the first time in the history of the Run, the Belgian Veteran Car Club entered a team of three cars, an 1897 Vallee, 1900 Georges Richard and 1900 De Dion Bouton Quadricycle. It was a vintage year for really old cars—the 1888 Roger Benz, L. D. Goldsmith's 1895 Benz, de Colver's 1896 Arnold and five other cars of the same year and no less than six cars dating from 1897. One of these was a Lanchester with George Lanchester at the wheel. Another, Denis Flather's Daimler, was to be commemorated for posterity on a souvenir envelope published to celebrate the RAC's 75th Anniversary in 1972. Flather himself was to carry a parcel of first-day covers to Brighton in the Daimler.

Bandleader Billy Cotton, in his younger days a good driver at Brooklands, beamed out at spectators from the cover of the 1959 Brighton Run programme, symbolic of the tremendous interest the Run now aroused all over the world. This year there were 249 entries, amongst them and officially representing the United States, a Locomobile Steamer, entered by the Antique Automobile Club of America.

'Just where do the cars keep coming from?' was a question many people asked as the entry list for 'The Brighton' continued to swell. In 1960, there were 263 entries, including cars from Belgium, France, Germany, Holland, South Africa and the United States. By this time, C. F. Caunter had retired and Philip Sumner was driving the Science Museum entry, in this case an 1899 Stanley Steamer. Jack Brabham was down to drive a Sunbeam but racing drivers were outnumbered by motoring historians, Bill Boddy, Cecil Clutton, Lord Montagu and the newspaper-owning Pratt Boormans being amongst the crews.

The police, who had a major task on their hands in controlling the vast crowds at the Run, were getting a little restive about the number of entries and, after talks with the RAC's Basil Tye, the principal organiser, it was agreed that in future the number of starters should be limited to 250. There were some police officers who wanted the start of the Run to be moved from London's Hyde Park to the outskirts of the City but the RAC refused to countenance such a suggestion and the idea was dropped.

Thus in 1961, only the first 250 entries to arrive were accepted. In subsequent years, entries in excess of this figure were to be accepted as reserves on the basis that some of the original entries inevitably dropped out. Thus it was possible to

'The Brighton'

always keep the number of starters around the 250 mark. The overseas representation was again strong in 1962 with cars from Belgium, Denmark, France, Holland, Italy and the United States. One of the oldest cars in the Run was an 1896 Panhard-Levassor, entered by the Automobile Club de l'Ouest and driven by the President of that Club, Monsieur Lelièvre. The Club also entered an 1897 Delahaye and an 1899 Panhard-Levassor Wagonette. American millionaire William Harrah, who owns a motor museum—and much else besides—in Nevada, was there with a 1904 Knox but the longest journey was made by Mr. and Mrs. Len Southward who brought their 1904 Wolseley from New Zealand to 'give it a go'. Len, a former holder of the Australasian water speed record, was 'bitten by the old car bug' in 1955 and later amassed a collection of some 30 veteran and vintage machines.

Next year saw the début in the Brighton Run of what is believed to be the oldest four-wheeled petrol-driven British-built motor car, the Bremer. It is said to have been built in 1892 although the Dating Committee of the Veteran Club contested this and officially labelled it, 1894. Either way, it had seniority on any other British-built four-wheeler.

The Bremer was the brain-child of a Walthamstow, London, plumber and engineer, Frederick Bremer, who apparently had access to the Benz patents and worked on the car in his spare time. The car was certainly a runner but apparently did not appear on the public highway after 1903. In 1930, Bremer himself presented the car to the Walthamstow Museum and in 1962, the Curator, himself a member of the Veteran Car Club, gave permission to John Trott and two fellow-members of the Club to restore the car and put it back on the road.

The Bremer's presence rather overshadowed what would otherwise have been the star attraction of the Run, an 1895 Rochet Schneider, entered and driven by Monsieur Henri Malartre, of France.

The Bremer was again entered in 1964 when, although that regular of the Run, Jack Brabham, did not return from the Mexico Grand Prix in time to take part, three other Grand Prix aces did—Jim Clark, Bruce McLaren and Chris Amon.

Clark, who had been robbed of the world championship in

a sensational last-lap drama in Mexico, was to experience another on the Brighton Run. Driving Lord Montagu's powerful 1903 Mercedes, he spanked down to Brighton in fine style. Then the engine spluttered and died within sight of the finishing line on the sea-front. Clark jumped out, put his shoulder to it and pushed the car over the line to the accompaniment of cheers from the crowd. 'I'm getting used to last-lap dramas,' was his wry comment.

McLaren and Amon made slower progress, having to stop frequently to fill their leaking Sunbeam with water. But they made it in the end, McLaren's second straight Brighton Run finish, something which gave the Kiwi, who was to die in 1970 in a tragic accident at Goodwood, great pleasure.

There was again a good foreign entry including a 1904 Laurin & Klement from Czechoslovakia. The driver, Moucka Frantisek, very kindly presented Lord Camden, Chairman of the RAC Competitions Committee, Dean Delamont, Basil Tye and myself with some Czech crystal brandy goblets to mark the occasion.

1966 brought another unique foreign entry, this time an 1893 Benz, entered by the Allgemeiner Schnauferl-Klub and driven by Herr Kurt Krannich. There were also cars from Belgium, Denmark, France, Holland, Italy, the United States, Czechoslovakia and Eire. Amongst the notable contingent, television commentator Fyfe Robertson drove a 1903 Fiat.

There were 282 cars entered for the 1967 Run and still older old cars appeared to lead the field, this time an 1894 Benz, entered by W. J. C. Ford. Norwich Corporation entered an 1899 Panhard-Levassor, indicative of the interest which many public bodies, including the National Trust, took in the event.

There was only one entry fewer in 1968 and, amongst the older cars was an 1896 Peugeot, brought over from the United States by A. and M. Helwig. Also from America came a 1900 Mobile Steamer, a 1901 Knox, a 1901 Locomobile Steamer and a 1904 Auburn. A 1904 Reo and a 1904 La Nef completed the strongest American contingent ever to take part in the Run. And for good measure, spectators could see Stirling Moss at the wheel of a 1903 Mercedes.

But the real surprise was reserved for the start when Prince Rainier of Monaco and Princess Grace appeared in car No. 128,

1. 'The world's first motor car'—the steam gun-carriage invented by French Artillery officer, Nicholas Joseph Cugnot, in 1770, is generally acknowledged to be the first successful self-propelled vehicle. A still from the BP film, *History of the Motor Car*

2. The first all-British designed and built four-wheeled petrol-engined car is generally reckoned to be the Lanchester, born 1895–6.

3 & 4. Arguments rage over the first American motor car. Reproduced here is some of the evidence for asserting that the Lambert, photographed in 1891, was ahead of both the Haynes and the Duryea

Walter Lewis, Ohio City, O.

5. The first motor show was held at Tunbridge Wells in 1895. Sir David Salomons (on left, at tiller) is seen demonstrating a 3¾ hp Peugeot

6. The Hon. Evelyn Ellis, photographed on October 15th, 1895, in the Panhard which he and F. R. Simms, founder of the Royal Automobile Club, introduced into Britain

## 'The Brighton'

a 1903 De Dion Bouton. At the request of the police, the Royal couple's participation in the Run had to be kept a closely-guarded secret beforehand and their bright red De Dion only arrived in England from Monaco the day before the Run. Princess Grace who as Grace Kelly was a well-known Hollywood film star, spent half-an-hour chatting with spectators before the start. The car crossed the finishing line at Brighton soon after noon and Prince Rainier said: 'I would love to go back and do it again.'

The Prince's mechanic, M. Robert Benit, said: 'We have nothing like this in Monaco. The Prince and Princess Grace were thrilled with the Run. I think they would like to do it again. I know I would. The crowds were "formidable" and the car went perfectly.'

There were 294 entries in 1969, once again headed by Louis Holland's 1894 Benz. There was also a Benz just one year older entered from Germany. New amongst the Continentals was a 1900 Jeanperrin from Switzerland. The Touring Club Suisse also had an entry, a 1901 Darracq. And a long way from home were Australia's Mr. and Mrs. L. O'Neil, with their 1903 Curved Dash Oldsmobile Runabout. Nearer home, the Herbert Museum Coventry and British Leyland entered a 1904 Riley Tricar.

What was often claimed to be the world's biggest motoring spectacle continued to grow and in 1970 there were 302 entries. Honour of being the oldest was shared by an 1895 German Benz and a car jointly entered by *Autocar* and Maurice Smith. This latter, a Lawson Steamer, was undoubtedly the more interesting of the two cars. It was originally built around 1895 by a Scottish postman and used by him for delivering the mail, hence the name by which it is sometimes known, 'the Craigievar Express'. The car has a vertical boiler amidships and a steam engine driving the rear wheels. The driver sits at the extreme rear and the single front wheel for steering is controlled by a lever. Stopping power is provided by brake blocks acting on the treads of the driving wheels. After all the work Maurice Smith put in to restore the Lawson Steamer, it would be nice to record that it reached Brighton in its début but, alas, this was not to be.

1971 was another landmark, the 75th Anniversary of Emancipation Day, and to celebrate there was an entry of 316 cars including one very special car indeed. This was a 1900 Daimler, owned and entered by Her Majesty the Queen. It was originally purchased by the Queen's great-grandfather King Edward VII and made history again by being the first car owned by the Royal family to take part in the Brighton Run. Rumour was rife beforehand that Prince Charles or Princess Anne might be aboard on the day but in fact the car was driven by Mr. Evelyn Mawer, Immediate-Past President of the Veteran Car Club, who had taken part in the Run every year since 1947 in his own Oldsmobile.

Motor museum support was especially strong this year as a quick run down the entry list shows: the Herbert Museum (Coventry), Het Nationaal Automobiel-museum (Holland), Solkoster Motormuseum (Sweden), and, of course, the Montagu Motor Museum. It would have gladdened the heart of motoring pioneer, St. John Nixon, who always swore that cars should be used from time to time and not allowed to moulder away in inactivity.

Nor were overseas entries lacking, 26 of them this time, including one from Australia.

So 'The Brighton' goes from strength to strength. There were 320 entries for 1972, ranging from the German regular, B. E. Rueckworth's 1895 Benz, three 1896 Léon Bollées and a Lutzmann of the same vintage, to a positive horde of 1904 cars. The usual star-studded entry list included Graham Hill, driving a car for Oxfam, and those top rally drivers, the husband-and-wife team of Erik Carlsson and Pat Moss. Television and stage star Dora Bryan was a passenger in Graham's car.

For the first time, the Run and a sponsor, Unipart, the British Leyland subsidiary which makes spare parts and accessories for all makes of cars.

Their sponsorship helped the battle against the rising costs of staging an event like the Brighton Run. Ironically, although the Run attracts many more spectators than any other one-day motoring event, there is no revenue from them, other than modest programme sales.

But such is the measure of support from all over the world, it seems impossible that 'The Brighton' should ever die as long as there are men—and women—interested in old cars.

CHAPTER FOUR

## To Love and to Cherish

The tall, elegant figure of Philip Fotheringham-Parker, racing driver, *bon vivant* and tough guy, settled itself comfortably beside the Long Bar of the Royal Automobile Club, one large hand wrapped around a glass of gin and 'sshhh—you know who'. In that familiar lazy drawl, came a casual question, 'Know anyone who wants to buy a veteran car? I'm thinking of selling my Lutzmann.'

'How much?' said I. '£5,000' said Phillip.

It was a figure which nearly caused some people to faint when I mentioned it to them later but, in truth, it was not a bad asking price for one of the world's rarest vehicles, only a handful of which exist compared with, for example, scores and scores of De Dion Boutons.

Yet, to talk of £5,000 in connection with any veteran car when it is remembered that the majority of them cost considerably under £500 when new, indicates that ownership of such a vehicle is a prudent investment in this day and age. Veteran cars may not compare, investment-wise, with houses, land or the Koh-i-noor diamond, but they are certainly in inverse ratio to the modern car which loses hundreds of pounds the moment you drive it away from the showroom.

And the prices of veteran cars continue to rise. I always remember another famous racing driver of yesteryear, Sammy Davis, telling me with surprise that an American had paid a four-figure sum for a Léon Bollée tricycle similar to the one Sammy himself owned and drove. The difference was that Sammy had paid 300 French francs for his—in the days when there were 120 francs to the pound!

One Norfolk farmer—and they know a good investment when they see one—was obviously convinced of the wisdom of his move when he paid £16,330 for seven old cars some eight years or so ago. Said Mr. William Milligan: 'These cars are in increasingly short supply and can't help but appreciate in value. They can be regarded as an investment like paintings or antiques.'

A simple illustration of how these cars can appreciate in value is given by a 1904 De Dion Bouton which as we said earlier, is by no means rare. One of these fetched £950 at auction. A year later, another of the same type, age and condition fetched £1,100.

So much has the business boomed that a number of very reputable firms now run periodic veteran and vintage car sales, amongst them Sotheby's, Christie's, Norman Cole and British Car Auctions.

As a guide to auction prices, it may be interesting to take a look at the first such auction staged by one of London's two leading auctioneers, Christie's, in July of 1971 . . .

Sixty-six lots were put up, four were withdrawn and, at the end of the day, only another four remained unsold. Those that were disposed of, raised £167,635 which, as Confucius once remarked, 'ain't hay.' It included a record price for a British veteran or vintage car at auction—£17,000 paid by Lord Montagu for a 1931 4½ litre supercharged Bentley. This was a rebuilt car, with a number of changes to the original specification, including a replica of the Le Mans four-seater racing bodies used on the 1930 Dorothy Paget-Tim Birkin team cars.

Nor was this a freak price. Two other cars changed hands at £15,000 apiece, one being another 1931 supercharged 4½-litre Bentley which, although not so attractive to look at as the one which Lord Montagu bought, did have an original Vanden Plas body. The other car fetching £15,000 was a 1930 Rolls-Royce Phantom II with original Barker four-door sports tourer body. A 1930 Phantom II with a replica body fetched only (?) £5,000.

But let us take a look at the veteran cars sold at this auction. Those built before 1905 and thus eligible for the Brighton Run naturally tend to get better prices than Edwardian veterans so, not surprisingly, the top marker was a 1903 Panhard et Levassor 10 hp rear-entrance tonneau, which, after being restored in 1967, took part in the re-run of the Thousand Miles Trial in 1970. It went for £7,000.

The Edwardians could not match this but still fetched tidy

## To Love and to Cherish

little sums: a 1910 8 hp Renault for £2,600; a 1910 20 hp Standard with an admittedly unusual French body, £6,000; a 1911 Daimler, £4,000; and a 1914 Belsize, £2,800.

If indeed there were any bargains, they were surely amongst the cars of the twenties where a 1928 Sunbeam went for £650 and a 1927 Essex for £700.

Compare those prices if you will with what was going on around ten years ago when top 'whack' for a Rolls-Royce was about £2,000 and eyebrows were raised when a 1910 Rover changed hands at £750.

One reason given by some for the increase in auction prices is the interest shown from across the Atlantic, but the Americans themselves dispute this, saying that prices in Britain have pro rata, outstripped those in the States.

Judge for yourselves. A few weeks before the Christie auction in England just described, a similar event was held at Radnor, Pennsylvania, USA. Here a bid of 66,000 dollars for a 1931 Duesenberg was turned down by the owner as 'being about 10,000 dollars short.'

Cars which were sold included a 1928 Du Pont convertible sedan, 16,000 dollars; eight-cylinder Auburn Speedster, 14,000 dollars; 1939 Plymouth station wagon, 1,400 dollars; and a twelve-cylinder Auburn Speedster, 20,000 dollars. Yet many other cars beside the Duesenberg were withdrawn and the general feeling was that the prices were too low.

Even if the prices are low by American standards, one cannot help feeling that advertising a forthcoming auction in Dallas, Texas, in British magazines was rather optimistic of the organisers. However, they introduced a practical note by advising potential British bidders that there were possibilities of arranging 'economy flight fares'. One cannot see this reversing the trend for European cars to be sold in the States rather than traffic the other way.

Obviously in Britain or the States, there is not much point in going to an auction unless you have bags of gold. So is there no hope of your joining the 600 or so people in Britain who already own veterans?

Yes, there is hope, slender maybe but hope nevertheless. Let us go back to fundamentals...

The days when all sorts of treasures lay hidden in barns, abandoned in fields, discarded at the back of garages and scrapyards, are gone. And, if indeed, you were still lucky enough to strike gold you will invariably find that you are no longer dealing with a simple-minded butcher only too pleased to take a tenner or two to get rid of the rubbish—but someone who knows the value of a veteran car as well or better than you.

Just the same it is worth following up any leads you get. Time after time, you may find that someone has beaten you to it; more often you will find that a 1901 Benz whispered into your ear turns out to be a 1934 Ford before your very eyes. The bits and pieces the farmer unveils for you may bear no resemblance to any motor car living or dead, known to man or beast. Although when this happens, you would be well-advised to make sure just what it is you are turning down before you actually do it.

Miracles can be wrought with bits and pieces. One car regularly competing in the Brighton Run was originally found in 'bits-and-pieces' state with the engine driving a potato chip machine.

In any case should the parts be genuine veteran parts, there is some enthusiast somewhere who would give his soul for them in order to restore or maintain another vehicle of the same make.

Short of the joy experienced by that miner in Colorado when his pick bit deep into the silver lode, there can be few delights greater than if your search is rewarded and you come up with a real find.

The first step in acquiring a veteran car, whether or not you eventually buy at auction, privately, from a dealer, rebuild scraps, or what-have-you, is to read the right advertisements in the right magazines.

For this purpose, it may not be unreasonable to say that two magazines are probably some distance in front of the others. One is the *Veteran and Vintage Magazine*, run by Lord Montagu, with the aid of Mrs. Ellen Broad and noted motoring historian, Michael Sedgwick. Its advertising columns may lack quantity but tend to make up for it in quality and often feature good cars for sale, both here and abroad.

## To Love and to Cherish

And should you not find the car of your dreams within its pages, at least you will have the pleasure of reading many interesting articles on the early days of motoring and on the history of many famous makes.

A regular contributor to the *Veteran and Vintage Magazine* is one William Boddy, who also happens to be the Editor of another somewhat unique journal, *Motor Sport*. In my own humble sports-writing days, they used to call Peter Wilson 'the man they can't gag'. In the context of motoring, Bill Boddy and his cohort, Denis Jenkinson, well deserve a similar title. This outspokenness carries over to the advertising columns which are almost as readable as the rest of the magazine. Indeed, I have heard people vow that they buy *Motor Sport* for the sheer joy of reading the classified ads.

Certainly you will find in the advertising columns, many veteran and vintage ads, including some from a number of established dealers who have earned a good reputation as specialists in veteran and vintage machinery. And again, as with *V & V*, you will find quite a number of articles and news items of interest on veteran and vintage matters.

*Old Motor* is another rewarding magazine in the field and so, oddly enough, is *Exchange and Mart*, if you are looking to buy a veteran. They are getting so much in the way of old automobiles through their columns these days that not long ago they telephoned for advice on the correct headings for the veteran and vintage advertisements.

*Old Motor*, an 84-page glossy magazine, is published six times per year but is also accompanied by twelve monthly news bulletins. To get both the magazine and the news letter it is necessary to join the Old Motor Club, 17, Air Street, London, W.1., the annual subscription being £5.00.

The Old Motor Club makes no bones about being a professional business as distinct from other clubs of a similar nature. Apart from the magazine and news letter, the Club offers books, posters, records and models at a discount from retail price.

In addition to the publications mentioned, you will occasionally find some veteran 'gems' in the more general motoring magazines, such as *Motor* and *Autocar*.

The second step in your career as a would-be veteran car owner is to join one of the non-commercial clubs concerned with the movement.

The Veteran Car Club of Great Britain, founded in 1930, organises events for classes of car made before 1919.

If your tastes tend towards later machinery, i.e., vintage rather than veteran, then the Vintage Sports Car Club is for you.

The beauty of both organisations is that although they naturally cater for people interested in veteran and vintage cars, they also cater for people interested in veteran and vintage cars but lacking one of their very own.

Associate membership is available for this category with full membership restricted to owners.

All categories of membership meet and mix together at club events and those fortunate enough to own vehicles are usually only too pleased to satisfy the interests of others and make them welcome at club events.

The advantage of joining one of these clubs *before* you secure a car of your own is obvious. You will get the Club magazine which, in addition to historical material, will tell you of cars and accessories and parts available, you will meet other people interested in the hobby and often you may be amongst the first to know when one of the club members wants to put his car on the market. Meanwhile, you can have a lot of fun attending the rallies and other functions which the Club arranges.

Full details of the Veteran Car Club and an application form for membership can be obtained form the Secretary, Mrs. Joan Das, at 14, Fitzhardinge Street, Portman Square, London W1H 8PL (telephone 01-935 1661). There are, in fact, three classes of membership: Full Members, who own cars and enter and drive them in events; Associate Members, who may drive Full Members' cars and otherwise share with them all the privileges of the Club; and Junior Members, children under seventeen years of age. In addition, Full and Associate Members may apply to become Life Members at special rates.

The subscriptions are modest although I will not quote here the rates prevailing at the time of writing since, in these days of galloping inflation, even non-profit-making clubs are forced from time to time to put up their rates to keep the wolf, or rather the bailiff, from the door.

## To Love and to Cherish

Application forms for the Vintage Sports Car Club are available from the Secretary, VSCC Office, Arnhem Road, Newbury, Berkshire (telephone: Newbury 4411). The vintage boys—and girls—have six types of membership. Vintage Membership is for owners of pre-1931 cars; Driving Membership for owners of thoroughbred cars of later date (up to 1940) and owners of historic racing cars accepted by the Committee; Associate Membership for those interested in vintage cars but for certain reasons unable to run one; Overseas Membership for those living overseas who are interested in vintage cars and enjoy receiving Club literature; Junior Membership for those under seventeen years of age; and Family Membership for wives of existing Members who may compete in Club events.

Later on, should you be successful in getting a car of your own, you will find additional advantages in being a member of one or both of these Clubs. They run special insurance schemes, registers of spare parts and libraries from which handbooks and other material may be borrowed.

Thus equipped with the appropriate magazines and club membership you are ready to hunt your veteran. Let us face it—if you have plenty of money there is little to worry about and the auction rooms, sooner of later, will provide you with the car of your dreams.

But if like most of us, your friendly bank manager is lurking in the cupboard, not to press bags of gold into your hot clammy little hands but to remind you of the size of your overdraft, then 'hunt' is the operative word. You are hardly likely to have the luck of Kent Karslake, the motoring historian, who found one veteran *complete* in boxes in a local garage and another mounted high in the air as an advertisement over a scrapyard entrance. But there are treasures still to be found as evidenced by the ever-increasing entry list for the Brighton Run. If you are really keen, have a go. I know the cars are there since twice in the last year the opportunity to acquire one had come my way.

For the moment, let us assume your search has been successful and you have acquired a veteran. With it you will have acquired two main problems. Firstly, what condition is it in? The only way to find out is to strip it down. In any event, it is almost certain to require some degree of restoration and, if this is to be professionally done, it may cost more than the original price of the car. Many owners have spent sums in the region of £5,000 to put their cars in showroom condition. The cheapest, most entertaining and sometimes most time-consuming method is to do it yourself. The time it takes will depend partly upon your own skill but also the availability of parts and drawings. This is where your membership of the Club will come in handy.

It is a moot point as to how far restoration should go. Personally, I favour restoration into original running-order so that the car may take part in events. Some people go further than this, chrome- or silver-plating parts of the engine and so on. It makes the car beautiful for display purposes and also reduces maintenance but to me, and a lot of others, it is a trifle artificial. However, every man to his taste.

Your second problem: is your pride and joy really what it is supposed to be? The early history of the motor car is obscured by the number of firms and people involved, the number of cars made under licence and given other names; the small output of some models; and the vagueness of owners concerning the history of their cars. So is that 1902 Whizanweze really 1902 or should it be 1900? Come to that is it really a Whizanweze or a Stopango? The problem is such a common one that the Veteran Car Club has what is known as a Dating Committee.

By checking the manufacturer's records (where these exist), researching the many volumes of motoring literature and by using an extensive dating bank they themselves have built up over the years, the Dating Committee usually arrives at the correct answer although it must be admitted that such research often takes a long time and the verdict is not always accepted by the proud owner of the veteran concerned. The Dating Committee's only interest, however, is accuracy and it is not unknown for them to change a dating when further evidence has come to light.

Apart from its significance to the value of the car and to motoring history, dating is not terribly important to the owner unless he wishes to take part in the Brighton where the upper age limit is, of course, 1905. Then, a decision by the Dating Committee that his believed 1904 car is in fact 1906 could be serious. But nearly all of the scores of other veteran events held in the British Isles are open to all veteran cars up to 1919.

## To Love and to Cherish

The rewards of being an owner are many. Apart from taking part in events at home, there are also boundless opportunities to go abroad for special events and the welcome given to the 'ancient pilots' is usually akin to that reserved for Royalty or Presidents or perhaps even more friendly bearing in mind the number of bomb-throwers and snipers lurking near presidential processions these days.

Then again there are plenty of invitations to appear in local carnivals and processions (if you like that sort of thing) and at the openings of shops and exhibitions. Always you will have to be prepared to answer a lot of questions about the car because the interest shown by the general public is quite fantastic. And so, sometimes, is the extent of their knowledge. Any hint that you will give a ride or two will bring a flood of would-be passengers.

The enthusiasm extends into high places. When the RAC's 75th Anniversary Exhibition *The Age of the Motor Car* was touring the country, veteran cars were frequently used to take the VIPs performing the opening ceremony to the exhibition venue. In Nottingham, Denis Flather's 1897 Daimler, also 75 years of age, was being used for the purpose. It is an open car and it was pouring with rain. An official tactfully telephoned the Mayor's Parlour and suggested that the Lord Mayor might prefer to come in his own closed limousine in view of the inclement weather. The answer was a very firm negative. The Lord Mayor had been looking forward to his ride in the 1897 veteran for weeks and nothing, but nothing, would deter him from having it. And roll up in the Daimler he did.

To end this chapter but not, I hope, your search for a veteran car, here are some useful addresses:

VETERAN AND VINTAGE TYRES

Tyres are the biggest problem facing the restorer of a veteran car, or would be if it were not for the famous firm of Dunlop. They are today the only company manufacturing a comprehensive range of tyres for vehicles of pre-war years. Although the production of Beaded Edge, Straight Side and Wired Type tyres entails many problems because they need to be hand-built in a mass-production age, Dunlop continues to manufacture them in

the interests of motoring. A centralised source of supply has been established and this is:
*Vintage Tyre Supplies Limited, Jackman Mews, North Circular Road, Neasden, London, N.W.10.*

RESTORERS AND REPAIRERS

The famous engineering group, Rubery Owen, the people behind the BRM racing car, also built the chassis for many an old car, and today provide a service for the renovation and repair of veteran and vintage cars and commercial vehicles. The address is:
*Rubery Owen & Co. Ltd., Repair Service Department, Meeting Street, Wednesbury, Staffordshire.*

For the restoration of veteran and vintage clocks, instruments and accessories, contact:
*John E. Marks, 4, Whybourne Crest, Tunbridge Wells, Kent.*

Providing a complete restoration service, including engine overhaul and body repairs, is:
*Goldhill Garage, West Avenue, Wigston, Leicester.*

Also offering a complete restoration, including ash framing, panelwork, etc., is:
*Vintage Coachwork, Highclere 253529 (evenings).*

SUPPLIERS OF PARTS, ACCESSORIES AND COMPLETE CARS

*Jack Bond, 20, Brook Mews North, Lancaster Gate, Hyde Park, London, W.2.*
*Raymond Radiators, 60, Chalk Farm Road, London, N.W.1.*
and also at:
*5, Ware Road, Hertford, Hertfordshire.*
*Clares, 260, Knight's Hill, London, S.E.27.*
*The Complete Automobilist Ltd., 39, Main Street, Baston, near Peterborough, PE6 9NX.*
*S. John Mitchell, Norton Mill, near Baldock, Hertfordshire.*

COACH TRIMMERS

*Connell Brothers, 693, High Road, London, N.10.*
*C. T. Laedly of London, 4, Grove Park Mews, Chiswick, London, W.4.*
*Roy Creech, 3, Wheathill Road, Annerley, London, S.E.20.*

## To Love and to Cherish

**REPLICA BODIES**
Specialising in replica bodies, although undertaking all kinds of restoration work:
*A. K. Bowley, Ashton Keynes, Swindon, Wiltshire.*

**BRAKE LININGS**
Brakes are always a problem on veteran and vintage cars. Specialists are:
*D. & M. Vintage Brake Lining Specialists, 47a, Manor Farm Road, Bitterne Park, Southampton.*

**MACHINING, ETC.**
For alloy welding, repairs to blocks, heads, crank-cases, camshafts, rockers, etc.:
*Liselotte Welding Service, 9a, Broadway, Bexleyheath, Kent.*
Cylinders rebored, crankshafts reground, etc.:
*Crankbears (Mortlake) Ltd., 17, Sheen Lane, London, S.W.14.*
For veteran and vintage mudguards, panel and experimental work:
*W. H. Broster, Bagley Street, Stambermill, Stourbridge, Worcestershire.*

**TRANSPORT**
Throughout U.K. and Europe:
*E. & E. Smith, Lower Green House, Green Lane, Hove Edge, Brighouse, Yorkshire.*

**GENERAL**
*Paul Beck, Brunstead Grange, Stalham, Norwich.*

**INSURANCE**
Insurance can be a rather tricky business where veteran and vintage machinery is concerned and in 1933, the RAC's official brokers, inaugurated a special scheme for members of the Vetteran Car Club, using their veterans for rallies and so on:
*Muir Beddall & Company Ltd., 37, Gracechurch Street, London, E.C.3.*
Others who can advise on insurance are:
*Vintage Car Insurance Associates, Hyde-East & Co. Ltd., 60, Chertsey Street, Guildford, Surrey.*

*The Book of the Veteran Car*

*The Association of Insurance Brokers, Craven House, 121, Kingsway, London, WC2 6PD.*
and
*The Insurance Manager, The Royal Automobile Club, RAC House, Lansdowne Road, Croydon, Surrey.*

The addresses given here are accurate at the time of going to press and give some idea of the services available to the veteran and vintage car owner. There are, however, many other firms and individuals engaged in various aspects of the business—the Veteran Car Club, for instance, runs a *Repair Service Scheme* which has about 200 firms on its books prepared to undertake work to veteran cars. Which is another good reason for joining the Veteran Car Club.

CHAPTER FIVE

# If you can't touch, just look

The owner of a newly-acquired veteran car will find a whole new world opening for him. But those who cannot touch can still look . . . thanks to the initiative and foresight of men who have gathered together the most wonderful collections of old cars.

Britain now has a National Motor Museum, due to the efforts of Edward, Lord Montagu. Sited at Beaulieu, Hants, one of the country's best-known and most visited 'Stately Homes', the National Museum has only come about after years of effort by its originator.

Lord Montagu opened his own motor museum at Beaulieu on a small scale, some twenty years ago, in memory of his father, a great motoring pioneer and a man who had ideas many years ahead of his time. Indeed, had he and some other motoring pioneers like Colonel Crompton been heeded, our cities and towns would not now be as congested as they are. At the turn of the century such men were suggesting flyovers, pedestrian precincts and off-street parking.

Getting back to the present, Lord Montagu long advocated the establishment of a national museum through the medium of a trust and this finally came into being with the establishment of the Beaulieu Museum Trust, a non-profit-making charitable trust set up to build and maintain Britain's first National Motor Museum. Backed by a large number of companies, motoring bodies and individuals, the Trust has achieved its aim and on July 4th, 1972, HRH the Duke of Kent performed the opening ceremony.

The Museum building is completely new and covers an acre of ground. The exhibits tell the story of motoring from 1895 to the present day with special displays and more than 200 historic cars, commercial vehicles, motor-cycles and bicycles.

## The Book of the Veteran Car

An adjunct to the Museum is the BP Motoring Library which contains approximately 2,500 textbooks, 7,000 motor manuals and 25,000 manufacturers' catalogues. The Library also has a photographic section containing 50,000 black and white photographs and 900,000 35 mm negatives of cars and commercial vehicles dating back to 1899.

The main Museum is divided into seven sections. The first of these is the Alcan Hall of Fame which commemorates the great motoring pioneers. Some, like Karl Benz and Gottlieb Daimler, were inventors of what might be termed basics, others like Sir Alec Issigonis were responsible for vital landmarks in the development of the motor car. Rolls and Royce gave their names to a new standard in luxury cars, W. O. Bentley became synonymous with the sports car of the twenties and thirties and Ford, Morris, Chrysler and Citroën helped to bring the automobile within reach of the masses.

Also commemorated in the Hall of Fame are some great racing drivers and record-breakers, amongst them Sir Henry Segrave, Sir Malcolm Campbell, Jim Clark and many more. In honour of these occupants of the Hall of Fame, designers and drivers, cars which highlight their achievements have been selected, including an 1899 Daimler; 1909 Rolls-Royce 'Silver Ghost'; 1913 Vauxhall 'Prince Henry'; 1915 Ford Model T: 1923 Austin Seven; 1924 Sunbeam Cub; 1957 Grand Prix Vanwall; and 1964 Austin Mini-Cooper S.

Next and most relevant to this book comes the Veteran Section which at the time of writing contains twenty-six vehicles, including the 1895 Knight; 1898 Canstatt-Daimler; 1903 De Dion Bouton; 1906 Renault; 1909 Humber; and—a flashback to an even earlier form of transport—an 1840 horsedrawn Gentleman's Travelling Chariot.

The third section covers Vintage and Post-Vintage Cars. The exhibits include a 1920 Stanley Steam Car; 1924 Bull-nosed Morris; 1924 Trojan; 1925 Rolls-Royce 'Phantom I'; 1934 Chrysler Airflow; 1937 Wolseley; 1947 Healey; 1953 Volkswagen; and the Triplex GTS Reliant Scimitar once owned by the Duke of Edinburgh.

Small but good is the Castrol Record Breaking Section. This has four world land speed record-breaking machines on display,

*If you can't touch, just look*

giving Beaulieu the edge over any other motor museum in the world. They are the 1920 350 hp Sunbeam, driven by Kenelm Lee Guinness and Sir Malcolm Campbell; 1927 1,000 hp Sunbeam and 1929 'Golden Arrow', both driven by Sir Henry Segrave; and Donald Campbell's 'Bluebird'. The 1920 Sunbeam and Donald Campbell's 'Bluebird' were the first and last British cars to hold the world land speed record and were, of course, driven by father and son, Malcolm and Donald.

Racing enthusiasts will get lost in the Ford Sports and Racing Section which contains thirty-four famous cars including a 1912 Hispano-Suiza; 1925 Bugatti Type 30: 1928 Bentley; 1933 Alfa Romeo; 1935 ERA: 1955 Mercedes-Benz; 1962 Formula One Porsche; 1966 Ford GT 40: the Lotus 49 of World Championship fame; and Jackie Stewart's March-Ford 701.

The Commercial Vehicle Section has sixteen vehicles, amongst them a 1907 Gobron-Brillie (often referred to as 'Gobbling Billie') Fire Engine; 1914 Albion; 1922 Maxwell Charabanc (which has been used as a Press bus on the Brighton Run); 1923 AEC S-type London bus; 1923 Aveling & Porter steamroller; 1939 Harrods electric van; and the magnificent Burrell Steam Showman's engine 'Lord Nelson'.

Last but not least of the Museum's main sections comes the Motor-cycle Gallery, dedicated to the memory of Graham Walker, TT rider, journalist and commentator and the Motor-cycle Museum's first Curator. There are no less than fifty-five motorcycles on display, among the more famous being an 1898 Ariel Tricycle; 1904 Rex; 1912 Norton 'Old Miracle'; 1913 Bat Combination; 1925 Sunbeam; 1928 Rudge-Whitworth; 1933 Brough Superior; 1937 Triumph Speed-Twin; 1961 Greeves and Bob McIntyre's 1962 Honda.

In addition, there are many other displays of working and static models, pictures, crash helmets and so on.

In opening the Museum, the Duke of Kent said:

'Exactly seventy-two years ago, in July, 1900, my great-grandfather, King Edward VII, made a historic—if somewhat brief —entry in his diary. It was: "morning—drive in motor cars". Thus was recorded the first, as far as I am aware, contact between a member of my family and the internal combustion engine. But what is perhaps of equal interest today is that the man who gave King Edward his introduction to the new pastime of motor-car riding was the father of the present Lord Montagu. Quite characteristically, the King embraced this new activity with enthusiasm, which seems to have been shared by Queen Alexandra, as she shortly afterwards wrote to her son: "I enjoy being driven about at 50 miles an hour . . . and I poke the driver violently in the back at every corner to make him go gently." Could my great-grandmother have been the original back-seat driver I wonder?'

An interesting sidelight on history, although some historians might quarrel with it. It is recorded elsewhere that in June, 1896, Frederick Simms, founder of the Automobile Club of Great Britain and Ireland (later the RAC), together with his friend, the Hon. Evelyn Ellis, demonstrated to the Prince of Wales (afterwards King Edward VII), the Canstatt-built Daimler car. This Royal demonstration took place in the grounds of the Imperial Institute and one of the tests in which the Prince was said to have participated was to be driven up a narrow wood ramp with a gradient of 1 in 10. According to the *RAC Jubilee Book, 1897–1947*, edited by the late Dudley Noble, this was the beginning of the considerable interest which His Royal Highness was to take in automobilism. If this report is accurate, it pre-dates King Edward's diary reference by four years.

There is also another instance reported of the monarch riding in a car prior to the instance mentioned in his diary. This occurred in June, 1898, when, according to the history of the Daimler Company, he took his first ride on public roads whilst staying with the Earl of Warwick. And others report a ride in 1893.

The world's first motor museum followed surprisingly quickly after these early forays.

Edmund Dangerfield, founder and editor of *The Motor* (as it then was), became alarmed at the way in which cars of historic interest were being broken up at what was a very early stage in the development of the automobile.

He acquired premises in the West End of London, formerly occupied by the big store, Waring & Gillow, and in June, 1912, *The Motor* Motor Museum opened in Oxford Street. Thirty-seven cars were on display but, alas, they were not to be left undisturbed for long. War was on the way. In 1913, the Museum

*If you can't touch, just look*

was transferred to Crystal Palace but in November, 1914, the space the cars occupied was commandeered by the Admiralty. The cars were hurriedly removed. Some were undoubtedly returned to their owners but others went missing and remained that way. Amongst these latter was the interesting Crompton steam car which Colonel Crompton had begun building whilst a schoolboy at Harrow. However, some of the cars did survive through the years and five of them—the 1895 Knight, 1895 Wolseley, 1897 Bersey, 1897 Pennington Tricycle and 1900 Wolseley—are today in the National Motor Museum. Thus, the nation owes Edmund Dangerfield a debt.

Until Edward Montagu opened his Beaulieu Museum in 1952, there was no Motor Museum as such in Britain after the dispersal of Dangerfield's pioneer effort.

The best that could be offered was The Transport Section of the Science Museum at South Kensington where successive curators did their best in limited space and with limited financial resources at their disposal, the Government being rarely disposed to lavish much money on museums.

Despite this lack of support, the Science Museum managed to preserve such unique cars as Evelyn Ellis's Panhard, the 1897 Lanchester 'Gold Medal' Phaeton, Bersey's electric car and the old Roger Benz which afterwards took part in a couple of Brighton Runs before being retired again after an altercation with a modern car.

Space limitations meant, however, that of about thirty cars in the Museum's possession, only about ten could be shown at any one time, the rest being in store.

In addition to those cars already mentioned, these include an 1896 French tricycle of uncertain origin, an 1898 Darracq-Bollée, a 1900 American Foster steam car, 1901 Daimler 'Kimberley' Voiturette, a 1903 Gardner-Serpollet Steam Car, a 1900 Rolls-Royce, a 1910 Swift and a 1913 Lanchester.

Incidentally, the 1897 Bersey Electric Cab was said to have been used to drive the Prince of Wales from Marlborough House to Buckingham Palace and back in November, 1897, so that Royal gentleman certainly did get around in the early days of motoring.

Thus, between the wars and in the immediate post Second

World War period, the enthusiast was limited in his opportunities of seeing veteran cars to the sparse selection at South Kensington and a November excursion to the Brighton Run. His only other hope was entrée to a private owner's collection or the rare chance of being allowed to poke into some odd corner of a car factory where half-hearted efforts were being made to retain historic vehicles, such efforts usually depending upon whether or not an enthusiast was to be found in the higher echelons of the factory management.

Today the situation is very different. Apart from the National Motor Museum, there is a goodly number of others, some municipally-owned, others private collections but open to the general public.

At the Science Museum, the long struggle has been won and the amount of space being devoted to motor transport is being increased.

This means that cars now stored at Reading and Knockholt will be on display in future and not hidden away in sheds on airfields. Not that airfields are to be sneezed at. The Shuttleworth Collection at Old Warden Aerodrome, Bedford, houses one of the finest displays of historic aeroplanes in the world and for many years, cars from the collection were regularly seen in the Brighton Run.

One veteran car collection well worth mentioning is the Herbert Art Gallery and Museum in Coventry. This concentrates on showing local products which is not so restrictive as it sounds, Coventry and its environs having given birth to more than a few bicycles, motor-cycles and motor cars!

Indeed, the original concept of a transport museum stemmed from a collection of bicycles given to the City.

I recall way back in 1957, speaking at the opening of the RAC's Diamond Jubilee Exhibition in Coventry, along with Alec Dick, then head of Standard Motor Cars, and, if memory serves me correctly, a very remarkable lady, Mrs. Hyde, who was then the Lord Mayor. Since those days, under energetic direction of the Curator, Mr. Cyril Scott, the Museum has gone from strength to strength and the present building was opened in 1960, the foundation stone having been laid in 1954 by Sir Alfred Herbert, after whom the Museum is named.

*If you can't touch, just look*

In 1972, the Museum housed the Jaguar Golden Jubilee Exhibition, 50 *Years—Swallow to Jaguar*. The permanent exhibits include a quite comprehensive range of cars. Alvis feature largely, of course. Coventry has the famous 1932 beetleback, the sole survivor of the 1920 Alvis Morgan-bodied two-seaters; and a much more modern Alvis, which was the personal transport of the firm's managing director. Jaguars are there too, naturally, together with rarer machinery like a 1913 Arden, a 1909 Maudslay and a 1911 Siddeley-Deasy. There is also a 1913 GWK, loaned by Leonard Lee, the former chief of Coventry-Climax and powered with a Coventry-Simplex engine.

Rovers, Singers and the less well-known Stoneleigh have their place and there is a rare bird indeed in the 1901 Payne & Bates Godiva. And, practising what they preach, the Museum authorities use as a runabout van, a beautifully-restored Singer van, restored one might add by the Museum's own mechanics after it had been found derelict in Leicestershire.

Bits and pieces are legion from Humber, Standard, Armstrong-Siddeley, Riley, Triumph, Hillman, Daimler, Lanchester and other cars associated at some time or another with the City of Coventry and there is even a Grand Prix Lotus of the Jim Clark era, which was powered by the Coventry-Climax engine.

There are some fifty motor-cycles and the fabulous aforementioned collection of bicycles, around 200 in all, which not only started the Museum but also set Coventry on the road to becoming a major transport manufacturing centre.

Not far away from Coventry is another city with a great claim to being the heartbeat of the British transport industry—Birmingham. The Birmingham Science Museum inevitably features the motor vehicle prominently—including John Cobb's world record-breaking 400 mph Railton-Mobil Special.

Of the privately sponsored ventures one of the best-known is the Cheddar Veteran and Vintage Car Museum, located at Cheddar, Somerset. The exhibits include cars, motor-cycles and the owner is never averse to loaning exhibits elsewhere if it will help the cause. The Cheddar Museum has the active support of the Veteran Car Club and the motoring organisations.

Another privately-owned is the Pembrokeshire Motor Museum, located at the Royal Garrison Theatre, Pembroke Dock,

Pembrokeshire. Mr. C. Chester Smith is the owner and like the patron of Cheddar believes in his cars being seen as much as possible. When the RAC held their 75th Anniversary Exhibition in Tenby, Mr. Chester Smith loaned a unique Arielette for display and also drove the local MP to the opening in a rather splendid Oldsmobile.

There is a Transport Museum at Hull which includes cycles, motor-cycles and cars plus England's oldest surviving tramcar; and the official Museum of British Transport, long located at Clapham but now split up with the rail exhibits going to York and the London Transport vehicles to Syon Park, Brentford.

It is a sad commentary on modern life that such a fine collection as that at Clapham should be split up for what appears to be nothing more or less than finance—or the lack of it!

The famous Sword Collection in Ayrshire was broken up upon the death of J. C. Sword but Scotland is still represented in the museum stakes by the Art Gallery and Museum at Kelvin Grove, Glasgow. The exhibits vary considerably but, for example, at the time of the Scottish Motor Show, the Gallery put on special displays of Scottish motor cars ranging from 1900 to modern times.

At Aberlady in East Lothian is the Myreton Motor Museum with around one hundred cars and motor-cycles. Some of these cars were originally in the Sword Collection and quite a number have appeared in TV series such as 'Dr. Finlay's Casebook.' Amongst the Scottish cars on display are a 1923 Arrol-Johnston, a 1927 Galloway and a 1928 Arrol-Aster.

With its great history of Tourist Trophy races, it isn't surprising that there is a Manx Motor Museum at Crosby on the Isle of Man. What may be surprising is that most of the exhibits have registration plates with the letters 'MN'. All Isle of Man vehicles must be re-registered with Manx numbers upon entry and the Curator of the Museum has done his best to acquire the numbers appropriate to the cars in the museum.

Another museum with a unique flavour is the Royal Armoured Corps Tank Museum at Bovington Camp, Wareham, Dorset. Here, as you would imagine, the exhibits include tanks and armoured cars from many countries, as well as Britain.

## If you can't touch, just look

A comparative newcomer is Wheatcroft's Motor Racing Museum at the old Donington Park Racing Circuit, near Leicester. Not a veteran, but one of the more modern cars on show has an interesting story. It is a GRD 372 in which Roger Williamson won the 1972 Shell-Motorsport Formula 3 Championship, gaining the chequered flag no less than 14 times. Lovers of older machinery will find at Donington many cars with much more history than the GRD. But possibly with not such a future.

The growth of museums centred on transport can best be judged by the fact that there is now an Association of British Transport Museums. Some are obviously rail or ship orientated but others feature the early days of motor transport.

Abroad, there were others of the same mind as Edmund Dangerfield, and *Veteran and Vintage* reader, H. C. Hopkins, points out that as far back as 1907 Paris Motor Show, there was a historical section which included more than fifty cars, most of them pre-1900. They included the world's 'first motor car', the Cugnot steam gun-carriage, La Mancelle and four pre-1890 De Dion Boutons.

The Society of Motor Manufacturers and Traders featured a similar exhibit in London in 1930 and Roberto Biscaretti di Ruffia and Cesare Goria-Gatti got together in 1932 with a view to arranging an exhibit at the Milan Show. This led, in time, to the establishment of the present magnificent Italian Automobile Museum on the banks of the Po. Some of the exhibits have had a little of their magnificence dimmed. In 1939, the Museum was found temporary premises in Turin but the coming of war meant that all tyres of the exhibits were requisitioned and replicas were not fitted until several years after hostilities ceased. And at least one car, a 1926 Itala racer, still bears the scars of shrapnel. Named after Biscaretti, the Museum is generally reckoned to be the largest and most imaginative in Europe. Naturally, Italian cars predominate including many rare racing models, amongst them the winning Itala from the 1907 Pekin–Paris race. There is also the progrenitor of Italy's illustrious line of automobiles, Bordino's 1854 steam landau.

Italy also has another museum—Padiglione Automobili d'Epoca, located at the Monza race circuit. Here and appropriately enough, competition cars dominate. The exhibits usually number around 30–40 and changes are frequently made.

France in many ways pioneered the automobile since although Benz and Daimler rightly get most of the credit for producing practical automobiles, it was the French who so developed manufacturing, sales and promotion, that the car became an integral part of the twentieth-century way of life. Motor racing owes its beginnings to the French and the French Automobile Club is the oldest organisation of its kind in the world.

There are, as a result, a goodly number of motor museums in France. At the Conservatoire National des Arts et Métiers in Paris, is the original Cugnot steam vehicle, 'the horseless carriage' which began the whole saga, and also the Bolleé steam carriage of 1873.

Much more off the beaten track is the Musée d'Automobiles Anciennes at Clères, near Rouen. This is owned by the Pichon family and includes some fifty motor cars plus a collection of motor-cycles. Amongst the Museum's earliest cars are an 1892 Peugeot and an 1894 Panhard-Levassor. Others include a 1910 Gregoire, a 1923 Soriano racer and, fittingly enough, some very handsome Bugattis. Much more bric-à-brac is also on display including posters of the Monte Carlo Rally. And if visiting museums makes you thirst or hungry or both, the Pichons run a hotel just across the way from the Museum.

The Musée Nationale de la Voiture et du Tourisme at Compeigne has as its star exhibit, Jenatzy's 'La Jamais Contente', one of the earliest of world record-breakers. It also includes a big collection of horse-drawn vehicles and steam carriages.

At Rochetaille-sûr-Saône, there is the Musée Française de l'Automobile with more than one hundred racing cars, motorcycles and cycles, some of them very rare indeed. There is another Musée de l'Automobile at Le Mans, home of the famous 24 Hours' Race. Here again there are more than one hundred cars including some early fire engines.

To the public museums, must be added the private collections. Champagne millionaire Fritz Schlumpf, for example, is said to have more than 200 Bugattis.

Germany, with more claim to have begat the automobile than any other country, has not been, perhaps, so progressive in com-

## If you can't touch, just look

memorating the fact. There is a museum which covers all forms of traffic very comprehensively and boasts the first Benz, of 1886 vintage. Otherwise the best collection is at the Mercedes factory in Stuttgart, the Daimler-Benz Museum. The exhibits here make it pretty plain that whether or not the Austrian, Siegfrid Marcus, the Englishman, Samuel Browne, or anyone else, first thought of a petrol-driven horseless carriage, Karl Benz it was, who turned the dream into a reality.

In Holland, there is the National Museum van de Automobiel at Driebergen. The rarities here include what is said to be the world's first six-cylinder car, a 1902/3 Spyker racer with four-wheel drive. The collection also includes private and commercial vehicles, posters, toys and accessories.

The Spyker, has, of course, secured the place of Holland in early automotive history, besides being 'the villain' of the famous film, *Genevieve*. The six-cylinder, four-wheel drive car was shown at the Paris Motor Show in December, 1903, and may or may not have pre-dated the Napier of S. F. Edge, announced in October of that year but photographs of which did not appear until early in 1904. The Napier was a production car whereas the Spyker was said to be specially-designed for competition purposes.

Be that as it may, the Spyker was unveiled in England in February, 1904, and was given test runs near Crystal Palace. According to *The Autocar*, the climb up Anerley Hill was 'more like an ascent in a lift than a run up on wheels.'

The National Museum, despite its name, is privately-owned and located not far from Utrecht, just off the Arnhem-The Hague motorway.

There are other collections in Holland—M. M. H. Lips, of Druen, estimates he has 300 veteran and vintage cars—and there is also a very flourishing Pioneer Automobile Club. Dutch drivers have been frequent visistors to England for the Brighton Run.

Austria's principal museum is the Technisches Museum für Industrie und Gewerbe in Vienna and here is the 1875 Marcus car, claimed with some justification to be the oldest surviving car with an internal combustion engine. Whether or not Marcus himself was the true inventor of the automobile is a subject

## The Book of the Veteran Car

which historians are likely to happily wrangle over for many years to come.

Even some of the more unlikely European countries have motoring museums. Sweden, who few people had ever heard of in a motoring sense until Scandinavian drivers started winning rallies, has the Skokloster Motor Museum and the Tekniska Museet, both in Stockholm. The former features Swedish cars, the latter cars, motor-cycles and aeroplanes.

Switzerland has the Schweizerisches Verkehrsmuseum at Lucerne which covers the whole panorama of Swiss transport, including the early Dufaux racing car; and in Portugal there is the Museu do Automovel at Caramulo, with a collection of veteran and vintage cars.

But for the biggest and most extravagant collections one has to go to the United States where private enterprise has resulted in some quite fantastic displays.

A list before me shows museums in Hot Springs, Arkansas; Los Angeles; Canon City, Colorado; Estes Park, Colorado; Longmont, also in Colorado; Southington, Connecticut; Yorklyn, Delaware; Washington, DC; Hialeah, Florida; Hypoluxo, in the same State; not to mention Miami, Sarasota and Silver Springs; Atlanta, Georgia; Chicago; Princeton, Illinois; Auburn, Indiana; Indianapolis; Cedar Falls, Iowa; Aberdeen, Maryland; Brookline, Massachusetts; Princeton, Massachusetts; Salem, Massachusetts; Southboro, Massachusetts; Dearborn, Michigan; Detroit; Holland, Michigan; Rochester, Minnesota; Camdenton, Missouri; Minden, Nebraska; Meredith, New Hampshire; Peterborough, New Hampshire; Bridgewater, New York; Centerport, Long Island; Greenwood Lake, New York; Southampton, Long Island; Cleveland, Ohio; Newark, Ohio; Allentown, Pennsylvania; Bethel, Pennsylvania; Huntingdon, Pennsylvania; Pottstown, Pennsylvania; Rapid City, Dakota; Piegon Forge, Tennessee; Castleton Corners, Vermont; Luray, Virginia; Natural Bridge, Virginia; and Lake Tomahawk, Wisconsin. They vary from Buckskin Joe's Antique Auto Museum in Canon City and the Smoky Mountain Car Museum in Tennessee to the staid respectability of the Smithsonian Institution in Washington.

Faced by such riches, it is difficult to know where to begin. Undoubtedly one of the most magnificent collections is located on

## If you can't touch, just look

200 acres of green at Dearborn, Michigan, in the heart of the Ford car manufacturing empire. Greenfield Village and the Henry Ford Museum together form the Edison Institute. Henry himself once said that history was bunk but you wouldn't know it from this collection which covers all aspects of American history with an emphasis on things mechanical.

Ford himself began the collection as far back as 1908 and the Museum and Village were launched in 1929. Apart from cars, hordes of them, the Village contains Ford's first workshop, the first Ford motor car factory and the bicycle shop where the Wright brothers began their flight to fame.

Amongst the cars, pride of place goes to the 1896 Ford Quadricycle, Henry's first car. Incidentally, there are two exact replicas of this car in Great Britain, built by Ford apprentices and valued by the Ford Motor Company at £15,000 apiece. One of them was featured in the RAC's 75th Anniversary Exhibition. Altogether there are around 200 cars in the Museum and the collection is not confined to Fords. They range from Roper's 1865 Steam Carriage to a collection of classic cars of the twenties and thirties, including the magnificent 1931 Bugatti Royale Victoria.

For no good reason that occurs to me, Arkansas is not the place where one expects to find collections of veteran and vintage cars. But it is. In the town of Hot Springs, for example, there are two motor museums, the Hot Springs National Park with cars ranging from a 1902 Holsman to a 1932 Cadillac, and the Mid South Museum with cars from 1900 to 1940. Then, in notorious Little Rock, the Museum of Automobiles, featuring 1965, at Petit Jean Mountain, some 65 miles from the now-the Winthrop Rockefeller Collection, was dedicated with some 38 cars, including a strong representation of racers. Included in the collection are a 1903 Napier, 1907 Renault, 1907 Rolls-Royce 'Silver Ghost' and 1908 Mercedes. The oldest exhibit is an 1866 Dudgeon steam vehicle, the newest a 1941 Packard Straight 8 touring car. The Rockefeller Collection was started in 1960 and based upon cars purchased from the estate of the singer, James Melton, who had a famous collection which, in his lifetime, was exhibited at Hypoluxo, Florida. Amongst the rarer exhibits are an 1897 Haynes-Apperson, 1909 Lozier, 1910

Simplex, 1915 Detroit Electric, 1917 Carane-Simplex and a 1925 Rickenbacker.

Reno, Nevada, is famous for divorces and gambling. It is also famous for Harrah's Automobile Collection. Harrah himself has taken part in the Brighton Run and his collection has been described by some authorities as 'the world's greatest'.

In quantity, there appears to be no doubt. At last count, the Harrah Collection numbered some 1,000 automobiles. The owner intends to get more so that when he regards the collection as complete it will encompass the entire history of motoring. At present, American cars predominate with a leaning towards Harrah's own favourite makes, Ford and Packard.

Quality? It is doubtful if any museum owner or curator takes as much trouble as Harrah and his staff in checking the authenticity of exhibits. This extends to checking every part of every car so that it complies with the original specification. If at some time in the car's history, the original carburettor has been exchanged for another make, for example, then the Museum will fit an original if they have it or advertise for one if they do not. In a typical advertisement before me, the Museum is seeking an oil gauge of a 1915 Briscoe, a transmission cover for a 1909 Ford Model T, an engine for a 1908 Franklin and axles and hubs for a 1904 Pierce.

There is another completely unique aspect of the Collection. Should you visit it, your admission money is refundable if you turn up at Harrah's Club in Reno within 24 hours.

Yes, William Harrah is a gambler who arrived in Reno after the war and built a gambling empire based on Reno and Lake Tahoe, known to television addicts as the location of some of the 'Bonanza' episodes. Harrah is confidently reckoned to be a millionaire several times over and his gambling rooms and automobile museum are said to have something in common— they are neat, clean and well-run.

'Greatest' or 'largest'? What is claimed to be the 'world's largest antique auto show' is not, in truth, a permanent collection. Every year for three days in October, the Antique Automobile of America holds its National Fall Meet in Hershey, Pennsylvania, home of the vast Hershey chocolate empire. Mem-

*If you can't touch, just look*

bers bring their vehicles from all over the States; more than a thousand exhibitors display everything from buckboards to fire engines; and nearly three thousand more sell automotive bits and pieces in the 'Flea Market'. The attendance is reckoned to be around 100,000 in total. The meet has been the subject of a thoughtful photo essay by auto buff, Ron Nelson, who says, 'No place else in the world is there such a gathering of vintage automobiles in terms of quantity or quality.'

These meets and nearly all the automobile museums and collections are fired by something more than commercial considerations. From them springs a world-wide network of enthusiasms, friendships and exchanges which makes the veteran and vintage car movement one of the more pleasant aspects of this sometimes grim old world of ours.

For instance...

An article I wrote for the *Veteran and Vintage Magazine* on the 60th anniversary of the Monte Carlo Rally brought me a letter from Mr. I. Mahy, of Ghent, who told me that one of the cars in a photograph used to illustrate the article was still in existence. 'It is the 1911 Delahaye which belonged to Mr. Paul Frot, living in Meaux, France. The body—"Double Berline-Obus"—was made on special order by Wantz-Meaux on an 87 type chassis. It runs on double detachable Michelin wheels at the back. The form of the body is very aerodynamical for its time.

'The car was found in 1955 when I bought it in Meaux from a scrapper. It was then in a very complete and rather good condition. The car is now for show in the Belgian "Kelchterhoef Automuseum" at Houthalen where 100 of my father's cars are stored.

'We still have the original "carte grise" on which the name of Mr. Paul Frot is noted and even the mention—Voiture de Rallye.'

Subsequently, and as a result of this correspondence, I heard from Mr. Eddy Soentjens, Director of the Houthalen Museum.

He gave me an interesting insight into just how such an automotive museum comes into being. His story began with a family named Mahy, the family of my first correspondent, who were boilermakers in Ghent. A son named Ghislain was born in 1907 and, as he grew up, became a keen mechanic. In 1924, at the age of seventeen, he built a motor car which he sold and with the proceeds set up in business as a car dealer. He prospered and became the sole dealer for the area for five leading makes—one American, one British, one Italian, one Dutch and one Japanese.

It was in 1944 that Ghislain bought his first old car—a 1921 Model T Ford. The seller was so delighted to get rid of it that he threw in an old motor-cycle for good measure. That was the beginning of a collection which was to reach more than 600 items.

But Ghislain ran into difficulties. He had this magnificent collection but nowhere to show it off properly. He met with little encouragement locally in trying to establish a motor museum. The Flemish Tourist League heard of this and stepped in. At Houthalen in Limburg, a mining village where the coalpits had long since closed, there was a magnificent estate, planted with fir trees. After long negotiations, a large plot of this land was allocated as a museum site, Mr. Mahy selected one hundred of the finest cars from his collection and one of the most interesting motor museums in Europe came into being.

Every vehicle, from an 1899 De Dion Bouton Tricycle to a 1939 Delage, is in working order. And there is an interesting story about almost every one.

For the 1927 Cadillac, Mr. Mahy had to travel to Norway to obtain the proper car doors. Then there is a 1921 Rolls-Royce 'Silver Ghost' with only 5,000 miles on the clock. It was purchased by a Dutch Count who intended to use it for a trip to Spain. But he fell ill in Brussels and died there. The car remained in a garage for 25 years until Mr. Mahy bought it—still in showroom condition.

A year older is one of the Daimlers which originally belonged to the British Royal family. It is faced entirely with snakeskin and fitted with cushions which can be inflated to suit the passenger's weight. Even more remarkable is the 1906 Lacroix-De Laville which had truly unique steering for, on sharp bends, the driver had to pass the steering column over to his passenger. Then there is a 1901 De Dion Bouton which was thrown into the Seine by German troops in 1940. Fished out five years later,

*If you can't touch, just look*

it was reconditioned and took part in several rallies before reaching its final destination at Houthalen.

The best 'believe it or not' story, however, concerns a 1913 Darracq.

Having discovered it in the Pyrenees, Mr. Mahy went there in 1952 in order to tow it back to Belgium with a large American car. On the way this latter car broke down and as it could not be mended on the spot, Mr. Mahy simply put oil and fuel in the Darracq and used it to tow the modern car back to Belgium.

The result of his efforts can now be seen in Limburg and it is appropriate that Belgium should have such a museum before it is forgotten that she too was once an automobile manufacturer, no less than 84 makes being marketed. Manufacture ceased around 1930 but some Belgian makes are still commemorated in the collection, amongst them several Minervas, the Rolls-Royces of Belgium; the Fondu, Charles Fondu being the first Belgian manufacturer in 1906; and a 1900 Vivinus, once the property of King Leopold II.

Thus in countries all over the world, however belatedly, steps are now being taken to remember the great engineers and pioneer autocarists who gave birth to a new and important industry which changed the lives of millions. Their work is being preserved for posterity before all traces disappear.

CHAPTER SIX

## *It isn't all gold that glitters*

There are some sidelines to the veteran car hobby which seem harmless enough to me but are likely to bring howls of rage from your dyed-in-the-wool, one hundred per cent purist.

Public Enemy No. 1 on their list is the man who manufactures modern replicas of famous old cars. Agreed such replicas should never be passed off as the genuine article and agreed they should never be allowed to participate in veteran and vintage rallies and other events.

Having said that, there seems no harm in people possessing them if they so wish. After all there do not seem to be enough genuine veteran and vintage cars around for those who want them. And, of course, a replica with a modern engine may be more suitable for everyday use than a genuine veteran.

Take, for example, the 3.8 litre Panther. This is not a true replica but rather an impression of the famous pre-war Jaguar SS. It is not only beautiful to look at—it is also, according to those who have had the pleasure of driving it, one heck of a motor car. So if you have around £4,300, why should a purist say you nay?

Then there is the Albany. This comes a little cheaper at something under £2,000. It looks a bit like the Ford which inspired it, has a dash of Fiat and Opel and uses a lot of Morris Minor parts. Designer Brian Shepherd said he always wanted a veteran car but could not find one at 'a sane price'. So he built his own, taking care not to make it an exact copy of anything, so as not to offend the purists. Whether or not he succeeded in this latter aim may be open to doubt.

Britain, not surprisingly, lags far behind the United States in the production of such cars. A 1901 Surrey has been produced there in large numbers, so much so that models exported

7. The 1898 Canstatt-Daimler, one of the two hundred historic vehicles in the National Motor Museum at Beaulieu

8. The front-engined Panhard was produced in commercial quantities, the first true indication that the motor car was here to stay (from the BP film, *History of the Motor Car*)

9. Famous racing motorist, S. F. Edge, with his wife and a friend, aboard one of the great motor vehicles of the early days, a Léon Bollée tricycle. Despite their flimsy appearance, these machines were very successful in races

10. The man who started Britain's motor industry, Harry J. Lawson and his wife, at the start of the first Emancipation Day Run in 1896

11. Herbert Austin, later Lord Austin, at the tiller of the first four-wheeled Wolseley car manufactured, which was designed and driven by him in the 1000 Miles Trial of 1900

12. H. W. Egerton, in his De Dion voiturette, a car of $3\frac{1}{2}$ horsepower, at the finish of the great 1,000 Miles Trial

13. Armand Peugeot brought his own Gallic flair to the new motor industry (from the BP film, *The Dawn of Motoring*)

14. The magnificent 1909 Rolls-Royce 'Silver Ghost' which has pride of place in the Alcan Hall of Fame at the National Motor Museum

## *It isn't all gold that glitters*

to this country a few years ago were as low-priced as £972. The Surrey was capable of 35 mph (the Albany does 40 mph) and had a fuel consumption of 70 mpg. More important, it complied with the Road Traffic Acts so could be used as ordinary transport as, of course, can the Albany and the Panther.

Based on the type of curved-dash Oldsmobile seen frequently in the Brighton Run, the Surrey really does have 'a fringe on top' which is just as well in the climate of the Western World. At least two firms in the States, one in Florida and one in Canton, Ohio, have manufactured these replica Oldsmobiles and there are other firms which will manufacture replicas to drawings of any veteran car, something which obviously can pose problems for organisers and officials of veteran events.

Surprisingly enough, one replica has been recognised by an official veteran car club. This is the Banner Boy Buckboard, made in Milwaukee, USA. The Antique Automobile Club of America has permitted this company to advertise in the Club magazine.

The Buckboard, is supplied in kit form and shipped exactly as it was originally, so the makers claim. The cost is around 400 dollars.

Star turn in the replica business is probably the Excalibur 35X, made at a factory in Italy and costing around ten thousand dollars. It is as near to a Bugatti as makes no difference and a joy to behold.

Even the availability of replicas still leaves a large proportion of veteran enthusiasts who are unlikely to have the wherewithal to acquire either the genuine article or an imitation thereof.

Which leaves models...

Models come in two kinds, the ready-made and those in the form of construction-kits.

Those who want to take the easy way out will find a wealth of ready-made models available and, without argument, many of them are beautiful examples of the manufacturer's art. Some are expensive—especially, in Britain, some of the metal-cast models from Italy and France—but others are remarkably cheap.

Amongst the low-price models, the Lesney 'Matchbox' series give the most fantastic value. Lesney produce models of all sorts of cars, moderns, racers, commercials—and these days quite a lot of weird and wonderful glimpses into the future of automotive transport. Yet, for enthusiasts their 'Models of Yesteryear' will always have pride of place.

In front of me as I write, or rather type, since my love of veterans does not extend to quill pens, is a selection of these 'Models of Yesteryear'.

I list them here, not as a complete list of the range, but rather to give some idea of just what is available. In no particular order, we have a 1911 Maxwell Roadster; a massive and beautiful 1938 Lagonda Drophead Coupé; a 1910 Benz Limousine; a 1907 Peugeot; a 1913 Cadillac; a 1910 Packard Landaulet; 1908 Thomas Flyabout; 1914 Stutz; 1911 Ford Model T; 1928 Mercedes Benz; 1909 Opel Coupé; and a 1930 Packard Victoria. There are many more in the range and, as one critic has said, the series has long since passed the pure toy stage and fully deserves to be classified as accurate scale models although obviously there have to be some omissions, bearing in mind size and price. If you collect these models, do keep an ordinary child's paint-brush handy for cleaning them. In these and other small models, dust tends to accumulate, especially on the seats and in the spaces between the engine compartment and the front wheel mudguards.

In addition to veteran cars, the Lesney range also includes such treasures as a 1925 Allchin Steam Traction Engine; 1911 'B' Type London Bus; 1907 London 'E' Class Tramcar; 1916 AEC 'Y' Type Truck; 1914 Leyland of W. R. Jacob & Co., the biscuit people; 1924 Fowler 'Big Lion' Showman's Engine; 1926 Bullnose Morris; 1908 Grand Prix Mercedes; and 1929 Supercharged 4½-litre Bentley.

Then there is an 1899 London Horse-bus; 1903 Duke of Connaught locomotive; 1920 Aveling & Porter Steamroller; an 1862 'General' locomotive, complete with cow-catcher; and a 1923 Type 35 Bugatti.

And more and more are being added all the time . . .

Very much in the same tradition but on the whole larger and more expensive are the Corgi 'Classic' models. More expensive is a comparative term since the Corgis too are most reasonably priced. On the whole they are more detailed than the 'Matchbox' models but—rather unnecessarily I feel—include plastic drivers

## It isn't all gold that glitters

and passengers in the appropriate costume. Deservedly popular in this range are the 1915 Model T Ford and the 1927 3-litre Bentley, victorious at Le Mans. There is also a 1912 Rolls-Royce 'Silver Ghost' which is fitted with a Barker 'Pullman' type body.

The more expensive toyshops may also have some foreign models, of which the best-known is the Rio range from Italy. Fiat and other Italian cars dominate the range and several items are an absolute joy for the collector, amongst them a very good reproduction of the 1907 Itala which won the Pekin–Paris Race. French cars can also be found, marketed under the title of Les Teuf-Teuf.

Probably first in the field in Britain were the famous Meccano Dinky Toys, although not all of these were replicas. For example, they produced a range of racing cars in various colours which were Meccano design and had never seen a race track. Nevertheless, Dinky Toys undoubtedly started many now middle-aged men on a lifetime of collecting model cars. In America, Tootsietoys performed a similar function and in Germany, the firm of Marklin.

Most of these early toys were made to a scale of 1:43 and this is the scale which still dominates the ready-made model market today. Why 1:43? There is a sound reason. In the 1930's trains were more popular than cars and the most popular gauge was 'O' which roughly corresponds to a scale of 1:43. Dinky Toys and others were originally introduced as accessories for model railways and so they were made to this scale so that they would not look out of place beside the locomotives and trucks and the miniature figures of porters, ticket-collectors and so on.

Ready-made models are, of course, available in other sizes, quite a lot of them 1:25, as for instance Politoys (who dabbled in sponsoring real racing cars), Togi and Schuco. The Italian firm of Pocher has produced models ranging from medium to large and in general scales vary from 1:10 to 1:86.

Oddly enough, those who want to put a bit more effort into their hobby and construct their own models will find an even greater range at their disposal ranging from plastic kits in profusion to heavy diecast metal models which are an engineering work in their own right.

83

In Britain, the most widely-known kits are the plastic ones marketed by Airfix, who also produce planes, ships and a variety of other models. Their veteran and vintage cars make up into truly first-class models despite their extremely modest cost. Models I have made myself from this range include the 1904 Darracq, which starred in *Genevieve*; 1905 Rolls-Royce; 1907 Lanchester Landaulette; 1910 Model T Ford; 1911 Rolls-Royce; 1930 4½-litre Bentley; and a grand old London open-topped omnibus. At the time I made these, all of them except the bus cost just two shillings from Woolworths and although prices have gone up since, Airfix still represent fabulous value. Incidentally, other cars now in the range, include the 1902 De Dietrich, 1904 Mercedes and the illustrious Bullnose Morris. Airfix also market paints, adhesive and stands for displaying models. And a more recent development are kits to make much larger models. The old Bentley has reappeared, this time to a scale of 1 : 12. The price has naturally risen with the bulk.

Revell are an American firm who moved into Britain as well and their kits too can be warmly recommended. They are indeed exported to some 78 countries. Models which have 'graced' the Drackett collection include the 1911 Maxwell; 1904 Oldsmobile; 1914 Regal; 1913 Mercer; and 1912 Packard.

Aurora and some other American manufacturers produce rather larger model kits which have some additional refinements including metal headlamps, bumper bars, windscreen wipers, etc. I have made up one of these and the result is impressive.

Kleeware Precision Miniatures are on a vastly different scale and make up into much smaller models than most of the others. Obviously the detail is not so good but nevertheless the range includes some very interesting cars and two in my own collection are the 1915 Model T Ford Sedan and the 1914 Stutz Bearcat.

In recent years, a great many Japanese firms have entered the business and thus the range at your local model shop is greater than ever before. Top of the class come the expensive metal kits which do of course repay the time and money spent when they are unveiled in all their glory.

Most of the plastic kits come with full instructions and are fairly simple to make up but there are some pitfalls for the un-

## It isn't all gold that glitters

wary and a few hints may not come amiss for those contemplating taking up the hobby for the first time.

The temptation to start assembling the parts right away should be resisted. It is usually best to paint them before assembly since if this is left until after the vehicle is complete it may be difficult to reach some parts with a brush and the whole effect will be spoiled if patches of unpainted plastic can be seen. There are exceptions to every generalisation and some simple models can be painted satisfactorily after assembly while on others a compromise is possible.

Take as an example, the Kleeware Model T Ford Sedan, a fairly straightforward model. It is essential to paint the interior parts first, seats, inside walls, steering wheel and steering column, since it would be impossible to do the job properly after cementing the two halves of the body together. But the uncluttered exterior can be left until after assembly and this has the advantage that a better finish can be obtained since no harm has been done to the paintwork in assembly. By adopting this method, you can also remove any blobs of dried cement or other blemishes before the bodywork gets the finishing touches.

Enamel paints should be used and not cellulose. Just about every colour under the sun is available from model shops and other stockists. It is best to have an assortment of brushes (ordinary water-colour paint brushes will do) using fine ones for the tricky work like the wheel spokes and rather thicker ones for the bodywork in order to get a smoother finish. If you can afford them, buy the best quality brushes. Cheaper ones tend to lose hairs during painting and the effect of what should be a smooth, gleaming surface is ruined if a strand of hair can be seen beneath the paint. If this should happen—and even the best brushes can lose hairs at times—then remove the offender with a pair of tweezers and paint over the affected part.

Always wipe your brushes clean after use and keep them soft and pliable. But however much you clean them, it will still pay to keep separate brushes for each colour and so avoid the possibility of an ugly black streak suddenly appearing on some pale blue coachwork.

Decide on your colour scheme for the whole car before you begin painting. A change of mind halfway through may result in a hideous clash of colours screaming at one another. The manufacturers usually suggest a colour scheme and this is often based upon famous cars which were painted in those particular colours. But the manufacturers can be wrong and you may get more enjoyment out of doing some research into the history of the car yourself before deciding on the colours. Or you may just like to pick your own colours and have a 'fun' car. Anyway the choice is yours and, after all, beauty is in the eye of the beholder.

With the paint question settled it is time to get down to business. Do not separate all the parts from the plastic frames to which they are attached until you are ready for them otherwise you may lose some small parts or find that you cannot identify them against the construction plan. Make sure that all the surfaces to be painted are free from dust and chips. The component parts of some kits are not cut out so cleanly as others so any extraneous plastic should be trimmed to the correct outline with a pen-knife, craft knife or razor-blade before painting.

A pen-knife is usually better for this work than a razor-blade as the latter tends to be too sharp and a slip of the hand can cause damage. Besides, a pen-knife is much easier—and safer—to handle when engaged upon tricky and difficult operations. Once you have performed major surgery, any minor obtrusions and erosions remaining can be smoothed down with a nail file.

The paint dries fairly quickly but just the same it is best to paint only one side of a part at a time, letting it dry completely before painting the reverse. It is advisable to paint those surfaces which will be inside or underneath the car otherwise obscured first of all so that when you paint the main exterior bodywork, roof and engine compartment, you can paint over any odd splashes which may have 'crept' round from the other side.

Should you be painting a completed model, always work with the model on bench, desk or table and not in your hand. It is steadier and safer and a better paint job will result. In painting the wheels on a completed model, lay the car on one side and paint the outer tyres, rims and spokes nearest to you and the inner side of the wheels furthest from you. Then, when the paint is dry, turn the model over and repeat the process.

## It isn't all gold that glitters

It pays to become a little Henry Ford and go in for some miniature mass-production. In other words, have two models going at the same time. Thus, whilst the paint is drying on one, you can be working on the other. This also applies during assembly when sometimes intricate parts must be glued and left to set firm before work can be continued.

Having painted all the parts or such of them as you feel should be painted before assembly, the operation of assembly and cementing begins. It is not really a major operation and any bright youngster from nine to ninety should be able to do it quite easily. Yet . . . as we mentioned before, there can be pitfalls.

The construction plans must be studied closely and in conjunction with the illustration on the packet of the finished model. Then you must check that all the holes and slots, connecting lugs and clips, are just where they are supposed to be. Sometimes a hole or slot has not been punched out properly or a lug has been broken off. If you spot these faults before assembling then they can be rectified.

Tools required? Very simple—a pen-knife, some tweezers and a bulldog clip or two. And you will not need these very often since most of the time your hands will suffice.

You will require a good polystyrene cement. This is normally obtainable in tubes and must be handled carefully as it sticks quickly and securely. It has to be used sparingly since to use too much will cause it to overflow on to the outer surfaces and spoil the appearance of the model. Should this misfortune occur, scrape off the cement with your knife and paint over. But as with so many things prevention is better than cure. Always apply the cement to inside surfaces only and use the minimum amount. It is much easier to separate parts and cement them again if you find them insecure than to clean and smooth and repaint a surface covered with hard globules of cement.

It may be a debatable point but in this connection think a little before deciding to fit windows and windscreens when these are provided. In some cases it may ruin the appearance of the car not to fit them but too often the cellulose screens do not look very natural anyway. It is extremely difficult to cement cleanly to the windscreen or window frames and trying to scrape excess cement from the windows often ends with ugly scratches or the windows coming away. Many models do not include these particular refinements and in general few lose from their absence.

Some very tiny or delicate parts may also be difficult to cement. The best way to deal with them is to squeeze a little cement on to a piece of paper and then dip the part to be glued into the cement, holding it with tweezers. It is much easier to judge the amount of cement applied this way than to try squeezing it from the tube on to the part. If you have large flat surfaces to cement together then hold them firm with a bulldog clip whilst they are drying.

Talking of delicate parts, be extra careful with mudguards. This tip came from a correspondent to *The Veteran Car Club Gazette* who pointed out that great care must be taken in selecting the right mudguards. If the wrong brackets of six seemingly identical ones are used the mudguards become lopsided. They have to be detached and this can be tricky, the brackets easily snapping. And herein lies a lesson. Never try to force a delicate part into its allotted place or you may break it. The steering column comes to mind as one part which often causes difficulty. Instead of forcing it trim the part so that it slides easily into position or, alternatively, widen the slot or hole. The former is usually the best method. This advice applies especially to the wheels and axles. If you make sure that the wheels slide easily on to the axles then they will revolve freely after assembly but you must make sure that no cement comes into contact with the wheel hole when you fix the hub-caps.

A final word on the practical side of models. When you lift them, always do so by the strongest points, the body and chassis, and never by wheels, lamps, steering column or some other part liable to 'come away in yer 'and'.

Before we leave the model-making and collecting aspects of the veteran car hobby altogether, let me recommend that you beg, buy, borrow or steal a book called simply *Model Cars* and published in Britain by Orbis Books at £1.25. It is a simple history of motoring, told through the medium of models by Edoardo Massucci, many of the models being from his own

## It isn't all gold that glitters

collection. It may not be the best of the many histories of motoring which have been written but the colour plates of the models, 114 of them in all, will show you just what is possible from this absorbing hobby. The cars range from Cugnot's steam carriage of 1769 to the 1934 Citroën sedan. The 1932 Rolls-Royce Henry Sedanca Coupé, a Pocher model to a scale of 1:8 and consequently measuring some 56 inches must, as the author says, be 'one of the most beautiful mass-produced models in the world.'

And there are many other delights in these pages. Simple but beautiful are the 1885 Daimler (a Wiking model: 1:43) and the 1886 Benz, same maker, same scale; and both, of course, representing the world's first practical automobiles.

Collectors with a leaning towards veteran cars, need not confine themselves to either the real thing or models thereof. There are, for instance, plenty of ashtrays bearing paintings of veterans or, better still, model replicas. The Lesney 'Matchbox' people market such items, including cigarette boxes, pen-holders, etc. You can take refreshment in a tankard bearing a veteran car reproduction (one of the firms producing these is Wade's, whose 'Veteran Cars In Pottery Range', authenticated by the Veteran Car Club, includes oil jugs, funnel vases, candy and cigarette boxes, tyre dishes and ashtrays).

Slightly more off-beat—and at odds with the drink and driving laws—are first-class reproductions of old car radiators designed as spirit flasks or decanters.

You need never leave home to collect veteran cars—on stamps. The number of countries issuing pictorials on the subject is steadily increasing and there are already enough stamps in existence to form a modest collection. Monaco, which like most of the smaller countries, reckons to gain a great deal of revenue from the sale of stamps and so produces far more than the natives will ever lick, has been quite prolific in 'veteran car' issues. These have reflected Prince Rainier's interest in the subject and, also of course, the Principality's involvement in the Monte Carlo Rally. In 1961, for instance, Monaco issued a commemorative set of no less than fourteen featuring a 1901 Fiat; 1908 Ford 'S'; 1912 Chevrolet; 1903 Rolls-Royce; 1894 Rochet-Schneider; 1898 Renault; 1898 Peugeot; 1899 Panhard-

## The Book of the Veteran Car

Levassor; 1900 De Dion Bouton; 1901 Mercedes; 1901 Delahaye; 1901 F. N. Herstal; 1906 Cadillac; and 1910 Buick.

The Rally has been commemorated every year since 1955 with the issue of a pictorial stamp and these have often featured veteran and vintage cars.

There is a Czech series of six telling the story of motor transport and this includes the first Czech steam vehicle of 1815 and the pioneer Czech motor car, the 1897 President. Neighbouring Hungary has also issued a set on the national transport museum and this includes the first Hungarian-manufactured car, the Csonka.

Most of the countries of Eastern Europe have issued motoring stamps at some time or another and there are even a few from some of the states which have disappeared in two world wars. In the West, the Germans have issued quite a number featuring motoring, amongst them a set on the 1939 Berlin Motor Show which included the 1885/6 Benz and Daimler cars.

The United States, not surprisingly, has led the way with automobile stamps, beginning as far back as 1901 and continuing to the present. The US Post Office Department believes in reflecting the American way of life and those who have contributed to its development. Thus, in 1952, the 50th anniversary of the American Automobile Association was commemorated with a stamp showing typical cars of 1902 and 1952.

There might be an additional stamp for your collection if the British Post Office held similar views. But, unimaginative as they are, they turned down flat a suggestion that the 75th Anniversary of the Royal Automobile Club in 1972 should be marked in this way. They turned down a money-spinner judging by the response when the RAC decided to 'go it alone' and produce a first-day cover bearing an illustration of Denis Flather's 1897 Daimler. Indeed, if first-day covers are your interest—and it seems to be a growing hobby—there have been a number of interesting British issues recently covering the major motor races and the London to Brighton Run.

Unfortunately, you will not find many veteran cars on Commonwealth stamps. The Postal Departments in most Commonwealth countries of what used to be called the British Empire are

*It isn't all gold that glitters*

apparently run by close relatives of the postal section of the British Post Office.

A final choice for 'veteran car' collectors. To commemorate the opening of the National Motor Museum, John Pinches, the medallists, have minted 'Great Car Ingots', the complete collection embracing 36 cars from the Museum. Alas, you may find it cheaper to acquire a real veteran car than these 36 ingots. In sterling silver they cost £6 per ingot, in 22 carat gold £100 per ingot. A good investment for a rainy day, presumably . . . since for once, that which glitters really is gold.

CHAPTER SEVEN

## *Stars on Sunday*

Pete Murray, Dinah Sheridan, Spike Milligan, Stirling Moss, Jackie Stewart, Jack Brabham, the BBC 'Blue Peter' television team and Princess Grace of Monaco all have something in common.

At some time or another, they have all crawled or bounded out of the blankets, according to their nature, at an unearthly hour on a Sunday morning to make the pilgrimage to Brighton in a veteran car.

It is perhaps not surprising that racing drivers like Stewart, Moss and Brabham have shown interest in 'The Brighton'—anyone of mechanical bent cannot fail to be interested in these grand old cars.

And other race drivers of earlier periods, people like Sammy Davis, John Bolster, Philip Fotheringham-Parker and Tommy Wisdom—are Brighton Run 'regulars'.

Prince Rainier too is a veteran car collector and enthusiast so it is hardly surprising that Princess Grace went along for the ride although, muffled and well-wrapped against the icy wind though she was, she did not seem so keen on it as her husband.

But what makes the film-stars and the disc jockeys, not to mention hundreds of thousands of folk in more prosaic jobs, so keen on veteran cars?

One good reason is a movie.

Now there have always been close connections between the Run and the theatre and silver screen since the first commemoration runs of the 1920's. Looking down the early lists of entrants one finds a 1903 Sunbeam which appeared at Drury Lane in *Wild Violets*; an 1899 Panhard which featured in the films *My Old Dutch* and *Beloved Vagabond*; an 1899 Liberty which appeared in the theatrical production, *The Forbidden Marriage*; a 1900 Peugeot, star of several films including *Those Were The*

*Days*; and a 1902 Peugeot which was in the Stanley Lupino film, *You Made Me Love You*, and was still living a glamorous life, being driven in the Brighton Run by 'B. Bira', pseudonym of the Siamese prince who in his pale-blue ERA was one of Europe's foremost racing drivers in the thirties.

Yet all these toe-in-the-water dabblings with show business were nothing compared with the impact which one single film was about to make. For when a South African-born producer named Henry Cornelius decided to make a film about the Brighton Run and call it *Genevieve* he started more than he knew.

As this is written in 1973, *Genevieve* is more than twenty years old, yet audiences from Wigan to Waggawagga are still rolling in the aisles and there is a constant demand from car clubs for special showings. *Genevieve* has been a tremedous box-office success. It made its stars—Dinah Sheridan, Kay Kendall, John Gregson and Keneth More. But more than that, it put the veteran car movement on the map.

Travel the world and you will find in country after country, veteran car club officials who will tell you that their organisation was struggling against apathy and indifference until *Genevieve* came along. Almost overnight, membership soared, offers of help in organising events poured in and so did hundreds of requests for information about veterans. In the wake of the film came the big boom in veteran car souvenirs—tankards, ashtrays, calendars, scarves and the like—and models, both ready-made and in construction kit form. At least two prosperous manufacturing organisations today founded their fortunes in the early days of the veteran car boom.

So what was so special about *Genevieve*? No one knows. Least of all those who made the film. In fact, no one was very keen on making it in the first place and it was only the enthusiasm of Cornelius, now, alas, dead, which got the project moving.

It was a typically British film with typically British stars. And, at the time, not particularly big stars. In the sequel, they all gave brilliant performances but, just the same, no one imagined that they would appeal equally to Mexican vaqueros and Middle East potentates, Australian sheep-shearers and Arctic explorers.

Some time afterwards, on the set of another film, I talked

with Kenneth More, by then a great international star, and asked him if *Genevieve* had converted him into being a veteran car enthusiast?

'Well, I didn't rush out to buy a veteran car, if that's what you mean,' said Kenneth, 'but I've always been a keen motorist anyway. I must have been six or seven when I learned to drive. We had a car called an Albert, which they stopped making in the twenties, and my father put it up on wooden blocks so that I could sit in it and learn how the controls worked. When we came to make the film, I had to drive a Spyker. It was a bit difficult at first but I had been so used to driving for so long that I soon got the hang of it. The major difficulty I found was in the braking. You know the brakes on these old cars are not very effective and it took rather a long time to sort it out. However, nothing happened to me like the things which happened to John Gregson who once ran into the back of a fire-engine because he could not brake in time.'

Enthusiast or not, Kenneth More remains one of the great band who will always remember *Genevieve* with affection. 'It did much more than make me a veteran car enthusiast. It made me. It was the turning-point in my career,' he says. From being one of scores of personable young men on British stage and screen, More suddenly found himself in demand.

The story of the film, as with most British comedies, was a simple one.

*Genevieve,* the true heroine, is a car, a 1904 Darracq to be precise, and her deadly rival in the film is a Spyker, of similar vintage. *Genevieve* is owned by a young barrister, Alan McKim (played by John Gregson), a rather solemn young gentleman who spends a lot of his time surrounded by spanners and other workshop paraphernalia.

His pretty wife, Wendy (Dinah Sheridan), comes to the conclusion that he cares more about the car than he does about her so she refuses to accompany him on the big event of the year, the Brighton Run.

However, the night before the Run, Alan buys her a new 'motoring hat', all is forgiven and Wendy exercises a woman's prerogative and changes her mind.

Unluckily, and as many real-life entrants in the Run have

## Stars on Sunday

often found, the journey to the coast next day is one long series of disasters and misfortunes. It is all the more annoying for Alan and Wendy because when they do eventually reach Brighton, they find that Alan's boastful and somewhat obnoxious friend, Ambrose Claverhouse (Kenneth More) has made the journey in spanking style in his Spyker. To add insult to injury, they have the greatest difficulty finding a room for the night, Alan having cancelled their hotel reservation after Wendy's earlier refusal to come on the Run. They finally end up in a dodgy boarding house run by an ogre of a landlady (Joyce Grenfell). The room is even more dodgy and has off-stage noises in the form of a chiming public clock located just a few yards from the bedroom window.

To cheer themselves up they go off to a night-club but it is just not their day—or night. Ambrose, at his most insufferable turns up with a beautiful girl, Kay Kendall, in tow.

She proceeds to get more than somewhat pixillated and in one of the most hilarious movie scenes ever screened she astonishes everyone by borrowing a trumpet from the orchestra and playing a solo *à la* Harry James before passing out.

Ambrose turns his attentions to Wendy and Alan resents it. Ambrose too is getting bad-tempered now that his rather less than honourable intentions where Kay Kendall is concerned have been frustrated by that lady's lapse into unconsciousness. Finally, the two men meet in *Genevieve*'s garage, Claverhouse makes rude remarks about the car, McKim gets furious—and the result is a £100 wager on which car will be first to reach Westminster Bridge on the homeward journey.

Alan's judgment has really got the better of him this time. The Spyker car is faster than the Darracq and the McKim family budget can certainly not stand the strain of finding £100.

But the wager has been struck and next morning the protagonists set off. Speed cops stop the Darracq but Wendy plays up to them and the susceptible men in blue allow the car to proceed. (This part really is fiction and, if you don't believe me, try melting a policeman's heart on the Brighton Road sometime. I don't give much for your chances even if your name is Raquel Welch.)

Fortunately, Claverhouse is having his troubles too. He is

delayed by a flock of sheep and when he tries to find a short-cut, the Spyker splutters to a halt in the middle of a ford. Ambrose's girl friend, very much suffering from the morning after the night before, has to take off her shoes and stockings and push —and Ambrose doesn't show much gratitude as he bellows orders from the driving seat.

By now both girls are heartily sick of their menfolk and their cars but Westminster Bridge looms up, *Genevieve* with one tyre flat and one mudguard missing, gets to the finishing line first and all ends happily.

Fifty-five veteran cars were assembled for the film—but one driver had no licence. John Gregson had to take hurried lessons which perhaps accounts for the 'coming together' with a fire-engine which Kenneth More mentioned. Actually there was no time for John to take the official test and so he was still officially an 'L-driver' when the film was made.

Another aspect of the film was not all that it seemed. Most of it takes place in brilliant sunshine. There have been sunny days on the Brighton Run but there have also been cold, wet and foggy days. Henry Cornelius took no chances. He manufactured his own sunshine with the aid of a high-powered generator and a few dozen arc lights.

Although John Gregson avoided trouble with the police, another actor wasn't so lucky. He played one of the speed cops 'seduced' by Wendy in the race back to London. He was fined two guineas for a traffic offence, going straight to the court from Hemel Hempstead where the local police had been teaching him the wrinkles of a speed cop's job.

The motoring organisations had a busy time during the making of the film, the RAC particularly so. Motorists kept complaining about wrong signs in the south-east and eventually someone tumbled to the fact that it was the fault of the film-makers. They were putting up their own signs so that bewildered motorists in country lanes forty miles from the coast suddenly found themselves confronted with a sign which read 'Brighton—two miles' or else went down a cul-de-sac under the impression they were following the signs 'To London'. A policeman was said to be especially irate. He found a sign outside his front garden gate saying 'Cattle Crossing—Beware'.

## Stars on Sunday

*Genevieve,* as we have said, soldiers on. The car itself is no longer in Britain, its owner having sold it to a keen collector in New Zealand. Recent magazine reports have indicated that it is now enjoying loving care nearer home in Holland.

Poor Kay Kendall, that bright flame which burned so briefly, is, like Henry Cornelius, no longer with us. Dinah Sheridan, after forsaking the screen for a long time for a real-life role as housewife, not long ago went down memory lane as a passenger in a car driven on the Brighton Run by the President of the Veteran Car Club, Evelyn Mawer. Afterwards she went to dinner at the Metropole, a dinner which always brings 'The Brighton' to a close.

John Gregson and Kenneth More remain familiar faces on stage, screen and television. What better way to end this brief dissertation on the stars who have taken the Sunday run to Brighton than to quote two stories which they recall from *Genevieve* days? John first...

The unit was on location in the Old Kent Road and, in a break from shooting, John was busily signing autographs for a bunch of youngsters who crowded around him.

'Say mister,' demanded a little girl of about eleven, 'was you in *The Venetian Bird?*'

'Why, yes,' beamed John, pleased that the child should remember him.

'Did you swipe Richard Todd on the back of the head?' the child then asked.

Still beaming expansively, John agreed that, yes, he had swiped Richard Todd on the back of the head.

'Then,' announced the child firmly, 'I'll never go to see one of your pictures again as long as I live.'

Kenneth More's favourite anecdote about the film happened some time after it was completed.

He told me, 'I went to America to attend the première of the film *Titanic.* They took me to see a show in which an Apache Indian, a very savage-looking man, fought an alligator in a pit.

'As we sat there watching, the Indian flipped the alligator over on its back, looked up at me and, in the most cultured voice imaginable, said, 'Excuse me, Mr. More, but did Kay Kendall really play the trumpet in *Genevieve?* I've always wanted to know.'

D

CHAPTER EIGHT

## *Oh, for a Bottle of Gin . . .*

It was one of those grey damp mornings when, whatever story the thermometer tells, the cold gradually seeps through the protective layers of flesh and starts to gnaw away the very marrow of your bones, when stamping feet leads one to the inescapable conclusion that far from warming them such exercise will only cause your toes to fall off, and someone quietly moans, 'If we had had any sense, we'd have put a couple of bottles of gin in the boot.'

It was, believe it or not, a joyous occasion. Britain had finally decided to take the plunge into Europe or, in other words, join the Common Market and to celebrate the occasion Lord Montagu, Stanley Sedgwick, the *Financial Times* and others had organised a 'Veteran and Vintage Drive Into Europe', the actual route being from London to Brussels, headquarters of the Common Market.

The start was to be from Horse Guards Parade, Whitehall, with the Prime Minister, Edward Heath, nipping out of the back garden of No. 10 to wave the starting flag from the podium of an RAC Service Centre. A handful of half-hearted Anti-Common Market demonstrators were hastily removed by the police to lurk rather meekly around the corner. The start was held for a few minutes to let the Horse Guards themselves trot by, at least one of their magnificent mounts finding the noise of a veteran car frightening and then, to a flourish of trumpets, the drive into Europe began.

The participants included a good cross-section of veteran and vintage cars and motor-cycles, commencing with the ubiquitous 1897 Daimler.

Then came the 1898 Stephens, 1899 Daimler, 1900 Napier, 1901 Pick, 1902 Beaufort, 1904 Siddeley, 1905 Rover, 1906/7 Coventry-Humber, 1907 Rolls-Royce 'Silver Ghost', 1907 Stan-

## Oh, for a Bottle of Gin

dard, 1908 Hillman-Coatalen, 1909 Dennis, 1910 Deasy, 1911 Rolls-Royce 'Silver Ghost', 1911 Rover, 1912 Iris, 1912 Sunbeam, 1913 Wolseley, 1914 Austin, 1914 Humberette, 1919 Standard, 1921 Horstmann 'Super Sports', 1922 Bentley 3-litre, 1922 Morris-Cowley, 1923 Humber, 1924 Wolseley Fourteen, 1925 Humber, 1926 Lagonda, 1926 Rolls-Royce, 1926 Swift, 1927 Rolls-Royce, 1928 Austin Seven Chummy, 1929 Bentley 4½-litre, 1929 Bentley Speed Six, 1930 Austin Seven, 1930 Lagonda, 1932 Invicta, 1934 Lagonda, 1935 Riley Nine Imp, 1937 Rolls-Royce, 1938 Morgan, 1939 Bentley 4½-litre, a fine collection of motor-cycles, eleven commercial vehicles, one of them complete with its own coal, and, just to reassure the rest of the Common Market that Britain was not living in the past, an assembly of modern machinery, Aston-Martins and the like.

'The Drive Into Europe' was a one-off special occasion event and there have been many others commemorating special events and anniversaries. For those enthusiasts who want to take every chance of attending veteran car rallies and competitions there are, however, quite a number of them held regularly. Membership of the Veteran Car Club will automatically bring you news of these. If you are not a member then you will find a fixture list printed in the *Veteran and Vintage Magazine.* Just to indicate the opportunities there are, the fixture list for July 1972 listed no less than 34 events, in places as far apart as Penzance and Dundee, North Wales and Forfar, Silverstone and Eastbourne.

Amongst the bigger events is the *Daily Telegraph*-sponsored Manchester–Blackpool Run which attracts tremendous crowds and has become 'The Brighton Run' of the North.

Launched originally in 1963 by the Lancashire Automobile Club and Blackpool Corporation, the Run was almost an instant success. Starting from the Town Hall at Manchester, the cars headed for Preston by the direct route for the older cars but with a diversion for those built after 1917. From Preston they went south to Hutton for a driving test at the County Police Headquarters and then back through Preston, Lytham St. Annes and Blackpool to the Royal Lancashire Show Ground with a *concours d'élégance* to wind up the proceedings.

Such was the attraction of the Run that in its first few years, the police estimated the average attendance at around one million and by 1965 there was an entry of 126 cars, all built between 1896 and 1930.

The organisers appreciated that the time had come for some extra help if the event was to continue to improve and expand and so they approached the *Daily Telegraph,* who have sponsored the Run ever since. The record is one of bigger and better every year. In 1972, there was the maximum permitted entry of 180 cars, including the oldest car ever to take part, an 1896 Lutzmann Phaeton, from the St. Anne's Motor Museum at St. Anne's-on-Sea, which is claimed to be the first German car imported to Britain, having been shipped across the Channel and landed at Portsmouth. Another Lutzmann, formerly owned by Philip Fotheringham-Parker and now the property of Bernard Garrett, was also entered.

These two Lutzmanns are the only two known to have been registered in the British Isles and both were imported into the country by a Mr. Koosens, of Southsea, Hampshire. A note in Mrs. Koosens' diary of 21st August, 1896, records that the first (the one now in the St. Anne's Motor Museum) had been sold and another of the same make ordered. The other was found in an open shed in Norfolk in 1930 and rebuilt by well-known enthusiast, H. J. Wellingham in 1938 and 1939. Fotheringham-Parker bought it in 1946 and ran it regularly in the Brighton Run until selling it to Mr. Garrett.

Other interesting entries included a 1908 Argyll Tourer, driven by the former Chief Constable of Lancashire, William Palfrey; and the 1902 James & Brown, known as 'Boanerges', which is the mascot of the City and Guilds College Union of London, and a regular participant in the London to Brighton Run. Rolls-Royce themselves entered the original 'Silver Ghost' of 1907, the car with a 15,000 mile run to its credit; and Kenneth Neve, the famed 'London to Edinburgh' model of 1911, which he found in 1963 and spent 5,000 hours restoring. The 'Silver Ghost' got its name from its quiet running, coupled with an aluminium-painted body and silver-plated metal work.

Elsie Tanner of *Coronation Street,* otherwise actress Pat Phoenix, has taken part in the Manchester–Blackpool in her

23.8 horsepower Sunbeam Limousine. She found it in a barn at Tattenhall, Cheshire, where it had been for 13 years covered with hay. Completely retrimmed by a former Sunbeam employee, it is thought to have been made for George VI when he was Duke of York.

Another event popular in the North, is the annual Trans-Pennine Run from Manchester to Harrogate, organised by the North Midlands and Yorkshire sections of the Historic Commercial Vehicle Club and the Transiclub of Rochdale and sponsored by the *Evening Post*. In 1972, more than 150 buses, coaches, lorries and fire-engines were entered for this, many of them representing Northern manufacturers such as Leyland, Albion, Crossley, Foden and Jowett. And, by the way, a Crossley tender of the First World War is now included in the Lesney range of 'Models of Yesteryear'.

Most of the vehicles in the Trans-Pennine, however, are around 40 years old.

The main annual attraction of the Historic Commercial Vehicle Club is their version of the London to Brighton Run which takes place in May each year. A truly wonderful collection takes to the road each year and the 1972 entry, for instance, included such gems as a 1910 Panhard taxi, 1913 Commer fire-engine, 1913 Thames omnibus, 1922 AEC 'S'-type bus, 1924 Tilling-Stevens lorry, 1928 Dennis 30 cwt lorry and a 1931 Sentinel steam-lorry.

For lovers of old racing cars, the Vintage Sports Car Club holds many exciting events ranging from hill-climbs at Shelsley Walsh to racing at Silverstone. And you will find plenty of people to argue that vintage racing cars look a lot more exciting than the modern cigar-tube.

Last but not least, if you are particularly interested in one make of car there are a number of clubs catering for one-makes. These clubs too hold regular events throughout the year.

One big advantage about most veteran and vintage events in a day and age of escalating prices, is that admission to the majority is free although the purchase of a programme (when available) will increase your enjoyment.

There is one more veteran car 'happening', for want of a better word, which does not fit neatly into any category. It is not a rally or competition, it is not a museum, it is not a collection of models. It is a building. Michelin House, in West London's Fulham Road, headquarters of the French tyre firm from Clermont-Ferrand.

Opened in 1910, it has dated even more than many contemporary buildings and it is doubtful if more than a handful of the many pedestrians and motorists passing by have ever spared it more than a cursory glance. Which is a pity. Because incorporated in the surfacing both outside and in, are ceramic plaques depicting great moments in the history of motor racing and outstanding drivers of the past are literally 'on the tiles.'

Charron, driving a Panhard in the Paris–Bordeaux race of 1900: Hemery in a Darracq in the 1905 Circuit des Ardennes; Thery's Richard-Brasier in the 1904 Gordon-Bennett race; the formidable looking German ace Lautenschlager in a Mercedes (what else?) in the 1908 Grand Prix at Dieppe; the elegant streamlining of Serpollet in the Rothschild Cup at Nice in 1903: Fiat star Nazzaro, also in the Dieppe Grand Prix; and Raggio (Itala) in the Circuit de Brescia.

The achievement of Minoia (Isotta-Fraschini) in winning the Targa Florio in 1907, his first season as a racing-driver, is commemorated. Another impression of the same race shows Nazzaro again in his giant 16-litre Fiat. Charron and his Panhard bob up again in Paris–Amsterdam; Fournier (Mors) in Paris–Berlin; Guilliame (Darracq) in Paris–Vienna; and Marcel Renault, Bucquet (Werner motor-cycle) and Farman (Panhard) in the same race.

The Chevalier René de Knyff (Panhard) is seen in the 1899 Tour de France; and on a more sombre note, the Race of Death from Paris to Madrid in 1903 is represented by Gabriel (Mors) and Louis Renault.

Victor Hemery's feat of endurance in driving from St. Petersburg to Moscow in 1908, a distance of 438 miles at an average of 51.4 mph over appallingly rough roads, is also noted. One of the plaques depicts Hemery's Benz with a couple of Cossacks galloping alongside. Presumably they were not able to keep up for long since Hemery must have got his car up to the region of 80 mph to average such a high speed as he did.

Why did Michelin commission these decorative tiles? You

## Oh, for a Bottle of Gin

must have guessed. Advertising was the same in 1910 as today—and all these drivers were at the wheels of cars shod by Michelin. Which presumably explains the absence of great British drivers like Jarrott and Edge.

So there we are. If you live in London and Brighton or Blackpool is too far for you to go to see those beautiful old cars, nip out next time you are caught in a traffic jam in the Fulham Road and take a look at the Michelin building. If London's property developers do not beat you to the site, of course!

Fortunately, Michelin tell me there is no chance of this and the tiles will definitely be preserved for posterity.

CHAPTER NINE

## *Look Back in Affection*

There is a common impression that the Brighton Run always takes place in a downpour. In fact, despite always being held on the first Sunday in November, the weather has been fairly good for many years and often the Run has taken place in brilliant sunshine, even if you could not fry an egg on the pavement. There was one occasion however when it rained from long before the start until hours after the last straggler had chugged his way into 'Sussex by the sea' and for me it provided the memory of the Run which has lasted longest.

It was 'one of those days' right from the start. My car was 'in dock' and since we live not far from Hyde Park, I decided not to bother to borrow one. Instead, with my wife and a colleague, I planned a gentle stroll to the start, doing our job of helping the Press and seeing the cars away and then catching a fast-trotting hansom cab to Victoria. After the Run, we looked forward to dinner in Brighton and a night out before catching the last fast train back.

We reckoned without the weather. We awoke to a steady beat of raindrops on leaves. Ever tried to get a taxi or hire car in London at six in the morning? Three very wet and very bedraggled figures eventually arrived at the start having walked a mile or so in an incessant downpour.

When we reached Brighton it was still raining. Working conditions were tough as rather naturally everyone, officials, Press and odd bods, tried to crowd into the two or three official caravans and escape the elements for a short time.

Worse was to come.

Southern Television were to present a programme on the finish during the afternoon and then came crisis. The commentator was taken ill. Drackett was drafted.

15. The 1913 Thames Coach, one of the unique historic vehicles on view in the Commercial Vehicle section of the National Motor Museum

16. Early motor-cycles and cars on display in the Houthalen Museum at Limburg, Belgium, a family collection which has grown into one of Europe's best motor museums

17. St. John C. Nixon, with co-driver Arthur Ayscough, and the Wolseley which he drove around Britain in commemoration of the 1,000 Miles Trial in 1960 and again in 1970—when he was 84

18. A 1901 Mors heads the parade of veterans waiting to start from Hyde Park in the annual RAC Commemoration Run from London to Brighton

19. HRH Prince Charles, with Lord Montagu, in the 1899 12 hp Daimler, the car in which his great-great-grandfather, King Edward VII, took some of his earliest car rides

20. A selection of vehicles in the National Motor Museum. Top: 1895 Knight, 1909 Humber, 1909 Rolls-Royce 'Silver Ghost', 1914 Vauxhall 'Prince Henry'. Centre: 1920 350 hp Sunbeam. Bottom: 1935 ERA, 1966 Ford GT 40

21. Kenneth More and Kay Kendall, complete with Spyker, in a scene from *Genevieve*, the film which put veteran car motoring on the map

22. John Gregson as Kenneth More's bowler-hatted rival in the film *Genevieve*. The car is a Darracq

## Look Back in Affection

The idea was that I should stand out in the open near the finishing-line and, from a monitor, describe the cars as they came in. Afterwards, I would walk along a line of interesting cars, interviewing their drivers.

We had a run-through. The producer had to agree with me that trying to describe cars from a monitor tilted towards the sky and with sheets of water running down it was impossible. So we agreed that I should do the commentary relying on the evidence of my own eyes and hoping the camera was picking up the same scene.

Meanwhile, the then Chairman of the RAC, Mr. Wilfrid Andrews, Lord Montagu and three or four other drivers had lined-up with their cars alongside me. They were already wet after their drive but they were getting more and more soaked by the minute.

The countdown began. Let Alan Weeks, an old friend and well-known BBC commentator, who was sitting in the warmth of his own home in Hove, describe what happened next: 'The programme opened with shots of rainswept Madeira Drive. Then the commentator's voice said, "Welcome to the finish of the RAC's annual commemoration run from London to Brighton." I just had time to say to my wife, "That's Phil doing the commentary," when the screen went black.'

It must have been the shortest outside broadcast in history. Subsequently it transpired that a land line at the end of Palace Pier had broken.

But Southern TV's Berkeley Smith came rushing along to me, 'Stand by and keep the drivers standing by. We're trying to trace the fault because we've got nearly half-an-hour before the programme is due to go off the air.'

Cutting a long story short, we never did get back on the air. The rain came down, I got wetter, Mr. Andrews and Lord Montagu got wetter, everybody got wetter.

Net result for me: a ruined topcoat, a new pair of shoes completely unwearable and—although it must have been an oversight—not even a letter of thanks from the television company.

We did have our dinner afterwards and we even went to the Sports Stadium and watched two periods of ice hockey before we all began to shiver with the first signs of galloping pneumonia and decided to head for home and bed.

Wilfrid Andrews had the last word: 'You can't say you've been in the Brighton Run unless you've driven down in the rain.' There was enough rain that day to last a thousand Brighton Runs.

Of course, everyone has their own memories of 'veteran car days'. Fred Bennett, that grand old veteran who was at one time President of the Veteran Car Club, recalled back in 1955: 'I have taken part in every Brighton Run but I have only once been disqualified and, ironically, that was because I got there too soon. It was the year the method of controlling the speed for the journey was introduced. I had left my mechanic to work out the times and keep me informed as I went along. Before I got to Westminster Bridge he told me that I was late, and again at Kennington that I was still later. I went faster and faster but at every point on the road he asserted that I was still late. The net result was that I arrived at Crawley before any timekeepers were on the job to check me. I went on to Brighton all by myself as I had gradually passed everybody in my efforts to keep time and I arrived at Brighton again before the timekeepers were on the job. When they did come they broke the news to me that I was over three-quarters of an hour too soon and consequently I was disqualified. Now I do my own timekeeping.'

Fred Bennett was one of this country's motoring pioneers and was awarded the Dewar Trophy by the RAC when, as the Cadillac agent for Britain, he arranged a demonstration, the first effective one, of standardisation of parts. Three Cadillacs were dismantled, the parts piled together and then three cars re-assembled from the heap.

As he moved into the eighties, Fred not surprisingly found the Brighton Run tougher going. More often than not, Andrew Polson, now Chairman of the Royal Automobile Club, would drive the car most of the way and Fred would take over for the final stage into Brighton. Even this was too much for him on his last Run and the game old boy had to be assisted into the Press caravan and given a 'reviver'. A few months later, he died in his room at the RAC's Pall Mall club house. As

## Look Back in Affection

Confucius once said, 'They don't make 'em like that any more.'

A contemporary and also at one time President of the VCC, was James 'Jimmy' Allday. His strongest memory concerned the 1933 Run: 'Eve, my 1898 Benz Dog-cart and I set out together on a bitterly cold day with a thick white frost. Over Westminster Bridge Eve became moody and I became worried. She was missing fire and just would not take any oxygen. We struggled on but after she had crawled over that precipice Reigate Mountain (or so it seemed) she finally came to a full stop. I decided that it must be carburettor trouble. The Benz carburettor is a vast copper pot containing about half-a-gallon of specific gravity petrol at the bottom, and into this is hung from the top cover, lamp wick, old rag, old socks or any other suitable old material that will soak the petrol up. I disembowelled the apparatus, which is cunningly hidden beneath the driver's seat, and the horrid secrets of our troubles were laid bare. The only wick was an old sock hanging into the petrol at the bottom of the pot, toe downwards—and that toe was a solid lump of ice, preventing the petrol being drawn up. Fortunately, I had started off on that cold morning with two pairs of socks. Removed the outer pair, fitted them into the carburettor and reassembled the whole caboodle. Eve then started up quite happily and we eventually sailed triumphantly into Brighton well within our time limit but with myself a little cooler around the feet.'

Ronald 'Steady' Barker, formerly of *Autocar* and now a free-lance motoring writer, has taken part in many veteran and vintage events all over the world, but he remembers vividly an occasion when he drove a Thornycroft in the Brighton Run: 'Just beyond Croydon, I changed into top gear with particular élan and suddenly found myself wielding the detached gear lever like a conductor's baton—excellent value for onlookers on the crowded pavements. Both handbrake and gear lever had apparently been rather inadequately welded in restoring the car to its original form after a previous owner's desecrations. A quick look at the brake lever confirmed that it too was 'semi-detached'. After nearly two hours, a small wayside garage equipped with drills as sharp as tennis balls had effected a temporary repair of the gear lever and fortunately the strong headwind on that day made brakes virtually unnecessary. If I had so much as touched them we should never have reached Brighton before sundown.'

*Autocar* writers have certainly had some tough luck on the Run. Maurice Smith's exploits with the Lawson Steamer are mentioned elsewhere and his successor as Editor, Peter Garnier, making his first Brighton Run, had to get out and push the car over the line. Peter had only just recovered from a serious illness and pushing cars, veteran or otherwise, is not recommended.

Some drivers—for example, the pilots of the giant-wheeled Lutzmanns—are reconciled to the fact that they will have to push their charges more than once during the journey. Former Brooklands driver Philip Fotheringham-Parker, wearing an Australian Army hat, has been a familiar figure as the 4 pm deadline approaches at Brighton, just getting in on time and on at least one occasion pushing.

How a Lutzmann driver feels has been described by E. S. Barry: 'You feel rather like an octogenarian octupus by the end of the day. The wick carburettor has no float and requires refilling every half-hour. The oil and water need replenishing three or four times on the journey. The engine stops frequently and the only way to start is is by pulling the fly-wheel over by hand. There are no foot controls so one hand is required for the throttle; another for the ignition; another for the air control which has constantly to be adjusted as the carburettor is very non-automatic; another for the steering lever; another for the brake and another for the gear lever which also acts as clutch by sliding the leather belts from fast to loose pulleys, because there are only two speeds.

'The Lutzmann, alas, can rarely be relied on to carry her passengers up any of the hills and usually they—and even the driver too—have to dismount and push. Her maximum speed is about fourteen miles an hour so there is no danger of exceeding the permitted limit but there is, at the same time, immense satisfaction in handling such a gallant old machine.'

I believe Courtenay Edwards, the distinguished motoring correspondent of the *Sunday Telegraph*, found out about the pushing part too late when he innocently accepted an invitation from Philip to be a passenger on the Run.

## Look Back in Affection

Owen Bridcutt, one-time advertising director of Iliffe Press and still hale-and-hearty in retirement—we were fellow-guests and neighbours at the 1972 Veteran Car Club annual dinner—culls his outstanding veteran car memory not from the Brighton Run but from a journey he made alone in his De Dion Bouton from the Midlands to his home in Hertfordshire. 'Except for short intervals, it rained hard the whole way, punctuated by a series of most violent thunderstorms. In spite of having no windscreen or hood I managed to keep dry and was thoroughly enjoying myself when, going up a long hill in the Cotswolds, I was overtaken by a large shooting-brake overflowing with humanity. The cheerful greetings and waving arms emanating from every opening indicated that the occupants were in very good heart. I noticed that they wore some kind of fancy-dress and concluded that a party of no mean order had taken place. Rounding a bend and continuing the severe climb in low gear, I was perplexed to notice the whole assembly bursting from their now stationary vehicle. My astonished eyes then beheld a troupe of morris dancers, all complete with rings on their fingers and bells on their toes. I was forced to stop and immediately became the centre of the dance. Never have I seen a more hilarious affair. When at last they desisted, the highest expressions of mutual goodwill preceded a combined push to assist my restart that almost rocketed me into the next county. Almost immediately I was enveloped once more in torrential rain and it was hard to realise that such a ridiculous occurrence had really happened. But it had, and I chuckled a lot during the remainder of that grand solitary drive.'

Another completely different 'veteran' experience was that of Commander J. D. R. Davies—at the shovel of a steam coach. 'In 1939, I was invited to take over the duties of stoker by my friend, the late Major G. W. G. Allen, on the first road trials (new series) of a great $2\frac{1}{2}$-ton steam coach which had originally been built in 1875. Being not without some experience in stoking, I gladly accepted, and found myself in a sort of nesting-box at the rear of the coach, behind the coal-fired boiler, charged with the duty of keeping a good head of steam, a good "glass", and changing gear when required. As the last process could take anything up to about ten minutes, it was, like marriage, not to be undertaken lightly or wantonly. Of course, as a good engineer, I was constantly busy with my oil-can. Fortunately, I could forget the cylinders: these were lubricated with suet. On that never-to-be-forgotten run along the Dorchester road from Oxford we were constantly assailed from astern by derisive young pedal-cyclists. Undaunted, my coachman (Major Allen) drew my attention to a little tap, neat but not gaudy, installed in a most convenient position. As the youthful ribaldry continued, my tormentors quite suddenly found themselves involved in a high-pressure jet of steam and water. Peace hath her victories no less than war.'

But the man with probably more tales to tell than anybody is the legendary S. C. H. Sammy Davis—famous racing driver and one of the 'Bentley Boys', journalist and for many years 'Grand Vitesse' of *The Autocar*, veteran car enthusiast and founder-member of the Veteran Car Club.

Sammy usually had his own Léon Bollée tricycle as a Brighton Run mount and on several occasions has had to push. Fortunately a Bollé is somewhat easier to handle than a Lutzmann but not without difficulties, nevertheless. The most epic of Sammy's runs with 'Beelzebub' the Bollée went something like this: 'We arrived at Bolney cross-roads and I had just remarked to my navigator, "The old devil's going like a two-year-old" when there was a nasty crunch and the engine died. Well ahead of time we thought little of this. Ten minutes later we thought otherwise. The contact breaker drive shaft had sheared. Now we had everything for dealing with the engine falling out, valves coming apart, bearings getting red hot, but nothing in the way of a spare shaft. For a brief moment we contemplated making one at the nearest garage with a lathe. Then the navigator said, "It will take an hour to make and fit that shaft. We shan't get to Brighton in time but if we start pushing right away we can just get in on schedule." Removing seamen's ponchoes, oilskin outer trousers, neck towels, fur gloves and the like, we began. We coasted down each hill, but some ill-disposed imp must have altered the gradients and stretches we well remembered as "down" suddenly became "up" and we got very, very hot for the rules specified no organised help and no towing. Our condition when finally we achieved the summit of Pye-

## Look Back in Affection

combe Mountain was pitiable and the temptation of various public houses thereabouts appalling but we went on pushing. How we got "Beelzebub" down past the Regent's Pavilion to the finish neither of us knew, being dead on our feet, but get the old sinner there we did—and within the time limit too.'

In contrast, John Ford recalls an occasion when his veteran wouldn't stop. 'It was the Birmingham to Coventry Rally when our present Queen, then Princess Elizabeth, started the procession. I soon realised that my Benz, one of the oldest cars in the rally, was not giving of her best and after the lunch stop my engine gave out completely. I resigned myself to waiting for my tender, in the drizzling rain that had begun to fall. As usual when one stops with a veteran, a crowd soon gathered and several people asked to see the engine. One very interested spectator plied me with many questions, particularly as to how the ignition worked. It was my salvation, for during the explanation I noticed that the sparking plug had unscrewed and completely disappeared. A spare was fitted and with a pull on the flywheel we were away but only with less than half an hour to arrive by the specified time. I am ashamed to say that I forgot I wasn't in a modern car with modern brakes and I found I couldn't stop on the wet road down the hill into Coventry. There was a policeman at the bottom on point duty. His hand was against me. I thought quickly and said to my wife, "This is one time when I knowingly have to ignore a policeman's signal." As we were commencing to turn left he must have seen my predicament and immediately stopped all the cross-traffic and beckoned me through with a large grin.'

One Brighton Run 'regular' who has taken part in veteran and vintage events abroad is C. W. P. Hampton, whose powerful 1903 Mercedes contrasts greatly with some of the more spindly old cars. But a chapter of accidents occurred when he was returning from a Mercedes-Benz Club Rally in Stuttgart. 'Forty miles out a front tyre bowled away into a cornfield. Soon afterwards, Bill Cook's 1909 Mercedes—running in company with us—burst a rear tyre and then two more in quick succession, necessitating an enforced night stop at Karlsruhe. Next morning we set off for the coast but after 75 miles of autobahn at 50 mph we too burst an irreplaceable rear tube. Two weeks later I flew back to Frankfurt where the car had been stored armed with spare tubes and other equipment to get the car on the road again. A replacement tube was fitted and after further delays caused by brake trouble and yet another blow-out, we finally left in pouring rain on our 360 miles journey to Calais. We suffered two further bursts—one on the Cologne autobahn and one in Belgium—before the trouble was located to the cavities of the rim-securing bolts and we remedied the snag by stuffing them with brandy bottle cork shims.'

Presumably an expensive but happy way of affecting a repair.

Red triangles are the recommended precaution when a car breaks down in darkness but Ernest Hare had a better method than that: 'In 1953, I made a journey of 875 miles from John O'Groats to Land's End with my son Geoffrey in my 1900 solid-tyred 6 hp MMC. On the fourth day the near-side half-shaft and differential pinion broke on the mountains so I went back about seven miles and collected an assortment of angle iron, bolts and other junk. I also bought about a dozen old cycle lamps. Putting these at strategic points around the car, we worked by their glimmering light through the hours of darkness until well after midnight. The broken parts were finally taken to Carlisle to be welded and then 400 miles were covered in spanking style without any mishap until four miles from Penzance, the offside rear solid tyre came off the rim. It was clipped on again by cutting grooves in the rubber and fastening wire round each spoke. The final 16 miles to Land's End were undoubtedly the bumpiest ride I have ever had.'

The *Genevieve* story, as already recounted, revolves around a wager made by the proud owner of a veteran car. It may have been fiction but it certainly had at least one real-life counterpart. Let Major M. W. Mills tell the story: 'In 1936, being young and very proud of the prowess of my 1901 twin-cylinder Benz, I accepted a small wager from a friend that I could drive my veteran from my home near Leamington Spa to Hyde Park Corner, a distance of about 90 miles, in less than 12 hours. It seemed "money for jam". The Benz was fast—about 25 mph in a favourable wind—and I thought reliable. I left home at 3 am with my friend sitting beside me. The candle lamps made no impression in the dark misty lanes as we hurtled along.

## Look Back in Affection

Suddenly a shadowy figure loomed up. A shout, a swerve—we just missed some village policeman on his rounds. No time to stop—in any case it was ill advisable. Apart from a brief stop at a garage to weld a fractured brake rod, all went well until Little Brickhill came in sight but up the incline the gearbox siezed. We stopped and removed the offending bearing which entailed taking off the front cylinder, the steering gear and radiator. We caught a bus to Bletchley, found a garage, machined a new bearing and returned to the car. By lunch time the whole was reassembled. After 200 yards yet another expensive noise. This time the main differential shaft had snapped inside the gears. Again everything was stripped down, welded and reassembled but after moving a few yards we came to a stop again. Time 11.30 pm. Attempt abandoned and two sad men returned by train.'

Back to that very wet Brighton Run with which we began this chapter. 'Andy' Polson and Norman Smith were taking part in Fred Bennett's Cadillac—an open car, of course. And the rain poured down on them with gusto.

Part-way along the route, they were halted by the traffic build-up and found themselves alongside a golf-course.

'Look, Andy,' says Norman, 'look at those bloody fools playing golf in weather like this.'

The rest is silence . . .

So the memories and the reminiscences come flooding back, some humorous, some dramatic, some downright embarrassing.

In the latter category was an occasion when members of the Antique Automobile Club of America came over to Europe in force. On the eve of the Brighton Run, they invited RAC Motor Sport Director Dean Delamont and myself and our wives to a party at the Café Royal. The invitations said 7 p.m. and we took this to be 7 for 7.30. We, that is my wife and I, arrived at the Café Royal at about five past seven and found, to our horror, that the company was already seated and just about cleaning up their soup plates.

Horror piled upon horror. We discovered we were guests of honour with seats next to the Chairman at the top table. Have you ever had to walk the length of a crowded room with all eyes upon you, 'The couple who-came-late to dinner'?

## The Book of the Veteran Car

Dear old Dean, whose unpunctuality is a byword in motor circles, and wife Judy, arrived even later, somewhere between the main course and the cheese.

Worse was to come.

The Chairman rose to his feet and introduced the main speaker of the evening—me.

Just another little detail which hadn't been mentioned before.

Even the best 'off the cuff' speeches are better for a little advance thought and this was not one of the best. My wife suffered agonies through it. So presumably did the Americans—but they at least had asked for it.

But they were all good sports and took it in their stride. I still wear the Antique Automobile Club cuff-links which they presented to Dean and I, along with bracelets for our wives. Come to that, I still drink from an AAC pewter tankard which Jack Lambert, one of their members, later sent me from the States.

Thus, hundreds of veteran car memories are filtered down to a few pages although some of these stories are being told for the first time.

And wouldn't it be funny after all these years, if Southern Television sent me a new pair of shoes . . .

CHAPTER TEN

# The Motor Car's Hall of Fame

The world must still have concealed somewhere about her rotund person, a whole treasure trove of veteran cars as yet undiscovered. Some years ago, as an advertising selling line, the magazine *Saturday Evening Post*, which ran its first automobile advert on March 31st, 1900, tried to compile a comprehensive list of cars sold in the United States since the beginning of the automobile industry. They came up with no less than 2,530 names and this remember is only for cars sold in the States. There must be thousands of other makes produced in Britain and on the Continent which never reached the American shores.

The *Saturday Evening Post* list included such exotic names as Beau Chamberlain, Ben-Hur, Black Crow, Golden Eagle, Van Dyke and Red Wing. Also some more prosaic ones like Red Bug, Zimmerman, Blumberg and Badger. All, alas, have disappeared into limbo and at the time of the survey only some 20 US makes remained on the American market—Buick, Cadillac, Chevrolet, Chrysler, Crosley, De Soto, Dodge, Ford, Frazer, Hudson, Kaiser, Lincoln, Mercury, Nash, Oldsmobile, Packard Plymouth, Pontiac, Studebaker and Willys-Overland. And one or two of those have since quietly expired.

Although manufacture has long since ceased for many of these old names, a surprising number of cars still survive, so let us flip through the alphabet for a glimpse of the fascinating history behind them.

'A' could be for *Apperson*, an Indiana firm of manufacturers who, in 1907, were advertising 'The Jack Rabbit'. Five thousand dollars brought you a guarantee that there were only 14 other cars like yours and they could all do 75 miles an hour, the car being based upon the same manufacturer's Vanderbilt Trophy racer.

Then there is the *Auburn,* also from Indiana, which first saw the light of day in 1900, having developed from the Eckhart Carriage Company, founded in 1874. Starting as humble single-cylinder cars, the Auburns later became quite exotic before declining in the thirties. Around two score other American manufacturers started in business the same year as Auburn—*Automote, Automobile Forecarriage, Automobile Voiturette, Auto Fore Carriage, American Power Carriage,* and *American Voiturette* amongst them—but most expired within a year or two.

The first letter of the alphabet is usually well-represented in the Brighton Run. The *Achilles* first saw the light of day in 1903, the makers being a Somerset firm, B. Thompson & Co. Ltd., of Frome. They were on the market for only a few years. The Scottish firm, *Albion,* later famous for heavy commercial vehicles began with private cars, their first appearing in June, 1900. The early models had twin-cylinder engines, tiller steering and solid tyres. Even earlier was another Scottish firm, *Argyll,* which started in 1899 and between 1905 and 1907 was reckoned to be the largest private car manufacturer in Europe.

The early Argylls had an unusual gearbox in which the lever went 'all round the wrekin' to select the required ratio. A couple of these cars usually take part in the Brighton Run and another is the property of the Royal Scottish Automobile Club.

The oldest engineering company in the world to produce motor cars was *Alldays* which came into existence in, believe it or not, 1650, although it is superfluous to mention that motor cars were not on their initial production schedule, their first car being manufactured in 1900. The oldest company to be associated with the Brighton Run from the beginning was *Arnold.* Their story begins in 1896 when the firm, full name Walter Arnold & Sons, of East Peckham in Kent, imported and sold Benz cars. They took some of these cars, modified them, fitted engines of their own manufacture and sold them as Arnold Motor Carriages, the first of them being driven in the original Emancipation Run of 1896 by Henry Hewetson. In later years, this same car was a regular entrant in the Brighton Run under

## The Motor Car's Hall of Fame

the ownership of Captain Edward de Colver, a charming gentleman who one always remembers as most co-operative to the Press and ever ready to do something to help the veteran car movement.

The earliest-ever Scottish car, ahead of the Argyll and the Albion, is believed to be the *Arrol-Johnston*, the firm being founded in 1897. The make continued in production until 1928 but the highlight of their history was victory in the first Tourist Trophy race in 1905. Some models had a most unusual three-cylinder engine with the central cylinder being of greater diameter than the other two.

The *Aster* came originally from France but chassis and components were sold to a number of English coach-builders and the finished products marketed under other names, amongst these being the *Whitlock-Aster* and the *West-Aster*. No one knows the exact history of the example which often takes part in the Brighton Run, it having been found minus coachwork and so, restored, it runs as an Aster although it may well have been an Anglo-French hybrid to start with.

The *Autocar* hails from Ardmore, Pennsylvania, somewhere around the turn of the century (the *Saturday Evening Post* says 1899, Denis Field of the Veteran Car Club 1900). Said to be the first American design to employ the shaft-drive, the private car ceased production about 1912 but the firm commenced making commercial vehicles in 1907 and have continued to do so up to the present. One of the two Autocars which took part in the 1972 Brighton was brought over from the States for the purpose.

Not so long-lived was the *Auto-Bug*. The manufacturers advertised to dealers 'There's good honest money in handling the Auto-Bug.' Unfortunately, the year was 1910, the unfortunate car looked like something designed in 1885, and the honest money went elsewhere. The Auto-Bug was born and died in the same year.

'B' is for . . . the *Baker Electric*. The Baker Motor Vehicle Company of Cleveland, Ohio, was one of the more successful manufacturers in the pioneer days, manufacturing electric cars from 1899 to 1916 or 1917. Baker Steam cars were made from

1917 to 1921. A little-known fact about the Baker Electric concerns one of the world's first anti-aircraft guns. A Dr. McLean, of Cleveland, invented a gun which he claimed would puncture an airship at $1\frac{1}{2}$-miles range, firing 200 shots a minute. In 1909, for demonstration purposes, the gun was mounted on a Baker Electric lorry. Military historians may know what happened thereafter.

A 1902 *Beaufort* which takes part in the Brighton Run is believed to be the only surviving example of the make but at one time the cars were quite popular. The company was a London one, which financed a German factory to build the cars Beaufort designed. They were in business from 1901 to around 1910.

Pride of place under this letter of the alphabet has to go, of course, to *Benz*. Siegfried Marcus may well have invented what we understand to be a motor car but he missed immortality by subconsciously or consciously not having sufficient faith in his invention. Thus the place in the hall of fame which might have been his as founder of the motor industry goes by fairly common consent to Karl Benz who produced his first motor car, a three-wheeler in 1885. Benz, in turn, did not move with the times, his cars showing very little change over the years and he yielded pride of place to Daimler. Meantime, a goodly number of Benz cars were made and usually five or six examples are seen in the Brighton Run. After the First World War, Benz amalgamated with Daimler to market the Mercedes-Benz and thus the two great German pioneers who never met in person, were at last united.

There is great similarity amongst some early makes of car and one of the reasons is that many of them were built under licence from Benz.

*Brushmobile,* American as it sounds, was in fact British, the Brush Electrical Engineering Company, of Loughborough, manufacturing cars for a few years around the turn of the century. One of their models, at least, bore a strong resemblance to the single-cylinder Vauxhall of the period. The American *Brush* was manufactured at a slightly later period, 1907–11, and was the work of A. P. Brush, designer of the single-cylinder Cadillac. At 500 dollars a time, the company claimed 'More

## The Motor Car's Hall of Fame

runabouts of Brush's design *are running* than of any other design in the world.'

Lots of other 'B' cars, especially in the States but although the *Buffalo Electric* was marketed for about six years, most of the others had very brief lives indeed.

One of the most famous names amongst the C's is *Cadillac*. The first 'Caddy' appeared in 1902 and the same basic single-cylinder model continued for the next six years. To Cadillac belongs the credit for the electric starter and elsewhere we have described their startling demonstration of the interchangeability of parts which marked a big step forward in the development of the automobile. Cadillac, of course, continued a great name in the automotive industry through two world wars and a depression up to modern times.

At the other end of the 'C' spectrum is the *Celer*. One model exists and no one is a hundred per cent sure of its origin. One theory is that it is a 1904 prototype made by Charles Binks, of Nottingham, who afterwards manufactured *Leader* cars. Opponents of this theory argue that as the Leader cars and also motor-cycles designed by Binks all have four cylinders, it is unlikely that the two-cylinder Celer has the same parentage. It is generally accepted, however, that the car does originate from the Nottingham area.

*Century* and *Century Tandem* vehicles were first made in Willesden, London, in 1899 and production continued until 1907. The well-known Aster engines were used although the vehicles themselves were—and are—rather odd-looking machines. Nevertheless, they were quite popular in their day.

Longer-lived were the French *Charron* or *C.G.V.* cars manufactured from 1901 to 1929. The firm was founded by the three great French racing drivers, Charron, Girardot and Voigt, hence the initials under which the cars were first marketed. In later years they became known simply as Charron.

Life gets confusing when one moves along to the cars bearing the name *Clement* and variations thereof. It is perhaps best to take matters chronologically. In 1898, Commandant Krebs, a director of Panhard et Levassor, designed a light car known as the *Clement-Panhard Voiturette*. This car was eventually sold in Great Britain as the *Stirling-Panhard,* just to complicate matters still more. Then in 1902, the firm of Clement-Talbot Ltd., was formed to market the French Clement cars in England and for a brief time the cars were sold as *Clement-Talbot*. Later they became simply *Talbot*. Meanwhile, in France, the cars were sold as *Clement-Bayard* or *Bayard*. Most of these variations on a theme are usually to be seen in the Brighton Run.

Another French hybrid is the *Corre*, first manufactured in 1901. If you detect a strong resemblance to Renault you are right since these cars were largely assembled from Renault parts.

Complete originals, despite the profusion of 'makes' in the early days, were not so plentiful as might be thought. A German hybrid was the *Cudell*. Max Cudell, of Aachen, built his first motor-tricycle in 1896 but it was based on the De Dion Bouton and made under licence. He opened a factory in 1897 and made cars based upon De Dion designs until 1904. Original Cudells were then manufactured until 1908. One of the *Cudell De Dion Boutons* is in Britain, the property of Mr. G. W. Rothwell.

Rarer still is the *Creanche,* which was made in Paris in 1899 to 1905. One was brought over from Switzerland in 1972 to provide the make's Brighton Run début. A feature was an unusual method of slackening the belt between the gearbox and engine so as to give the effect of a clutch. A lever slides the entire engine back a fraction. The firm also produced electric cars at one time.

Lost in the mists of time, alas, is the *Chelsea,* a car marketed between 1901 and 1904. Along with it have gone the *Chicago, Chatham, Champion Electric* and many more, including the remarkable *Carter Twin-Engine,* manufactured in 1908 by Carter Motor Corporation of Washington, DC. It had two of everything, engines, batteries, carburettors, clutches, etc. The engines could be used together or separately and thus, it was claimed, the car gave 100 per cent reliability and the driver had nothing to fear from breakdowns. Unfortunately, what seemed like a bright idea had a very short life. The Carter cost five thousand dollars which was not exactly cheap at the time and presumably cost is the reason no manufacturer has revived the idea

## The Motor Car's Hall of Fame

since, except of course, in terms of record-breakers with more than one engine.

On to the next letter of the alphabet where pride of place naturally goes to *Daimler*. The English Daimler Company had no direct connection with the German firm, other than that both started as a consequence of Gottlieb Daimler's invention of the high-speed engine in 1885.

The English company came into existence in 1896 and manufactured engines. The following year, it began manufacture of complete cars, largely based upon the successful French Panhard cars which themselves owed something to Daimler's invention.

Another illustrious name is that of *De Dion Bouton*. Two names would be a more apt description since the firm was founded by a man who might claim to be the first racing motorist of them all, the Comte de Dion, and Monsieur Bouton. Their early vehicles were steam-driven, one of them winning second prize in the 1894 Paris–Rouen event, and later they made petrol-driven tricycles, followed by rear-engined voiturettes (oh, my Morris and my Minor long ago.) The first front-engined De Dion was produced in 1901 and a variety of models followed, including two-cylinder, four-cylinder and V8's. Production of both private and commercial vehicles continued until the 1930's and, indeed, one of my childhood memories is of the De Dion factory which used to be located near to the Swan & Pyramids at the 'border' of North Finchley and Whetstone, Middlesex, and which during the Second World War was taken over by a firm engaged in essential production. De Dion Bouton engines were also sold in large quantities to the manufacturers of other cars who wanted to fit a well-known engine rather than develop one of their own. The quality of De Dion Bouton design and workmanship is evidenced by the fact that more veterans of this make are in existence today than any other and the Brighton Run alone usually sees something like fifty or sixty cars running under the De Dion banner.

Yet it would be hard to dispute that *Darracq* is almost as famous a name as De Dion or Daimler. One of the earliest French companies, Darracq was founded about 1896 (what a vintage year for automobilism that was) and their first 'conventional' motor car was produced about 1900. For many years a standard feature was the gear-change lever mounted just under the steering-wheel and the make did establish quite a reputation in racing circles.

Another well-known French firm was that of *Decauville* which started as a manufacturer of locomotives but expanded to car production in 1898. From the outset, Decauville cars were fitted with independent front suspension which makes one wonder how many pioneer inventors have not had due recognition and how many 'Johnny-come-latelys' have received the credit which really belonged to others?

A third French firm of the time was *De Dietrich*, which enjoyed a great deal of success in racing circles for a good number of years after its foundation in 1898.

Two years earlier came the founding of yet another French concern whose racing successes were to extend over several decades, *Delahaye*. The Delahaye story began in 1896 with a horizontal-engined, belt and chain transmission car and continued through various changes right up until 1954.

Still in existence today are some of the early Belgian *Delin* cars. This firm made voiturettes and motor-cycles during 1899–1901 and in the latter year produced a light car, powered by a Kelecom engine. Two of these took part in the 1972 Brighton Run.

A contemporaty German manufacturer was *Durkopp*. These cars have appeared under other names in England—in 1901 as *Cannello-Durkopp* and the following year as *Watsonia*, later to become famous as a make of motor-cycle side-car. The Durkopp cars, and variations thereof, were very much akin to the French Panhards.

Many people are surprised to know that one of the earliest car manufacturers was the firm of *Dennis*, which became famous in later years as a manufacturer of fire-engines and commercial vehicles. But, in fact, Dennis commenced early in the twentieth century by making cycles, motor-cycles, quadricycles and cars. The cars, noted for worm-drive, continued in production until 1915.

Generally accepted as the oldest American car is the *Duryea*, which was built between 1892 and 1914, and had the honour of taking part in the first Brighton Run in 1896. This car, the invention of two brothers, was accepted as the pioneer of the US automobile industry after a rival claim by Elwood *Haynes* had been discounted.

Later it appeared that there was more substance to the Haynes claim than many people thought. It came to light that a year before the Duryea made its début, John William *Lambert* was driving a petrol-engined car on the streets of Ohio City, Ohio. This was substantiated by witnesses who either rode in or saw the car. Why did Lambert never press his claim for recognition?

He was unable to launch the car on a successful sales basis and decided that there was no immediate market for motor cars. which would show a profit. When Haynes, a friend of Lambert, launched his car he sought permission from John William to advertise the Haynes as America's first. This permission was forthcoming and in later years, Lambert steadfastly refused to be drawn into the Duryea v. Haynes controversy. He became a successful manufacturer of cars, trucks, fire-engines and tractors and today, Lambert Incorporated, still a family business, has factories at Daytona and Ansonia, Ohio, where automotive parts, production machine tools and lawn and industrial sweepers are made.

Lambert himself seemed contented with the credit given him in history books as 'the father of the gearless, friction-drive engine as applied to the automobile.'

Also among the many scores of 'Ds' and worthy of mention is the *Dechamps*. This was another Belgian make, the firm starting with tricycles and then going on to more conventional cars.

Turning to 'E' one finds what is probably the most remarkable of British cars, the *English Mechanic*. At the turn of the century, a journal known as *The English Mechanic and World of Science* published a series of articles to enable its readers to construct their own motor cars—do-it-yourself in one of its earliest versions. A number of different designs appeared and one car which takes part in the Brighton Run quite often follows closely upon a 1900 design which itself was very much akin to the then Benz layout. Another Brighton Run contestant is based upon a design published in 1904.

Also unusual is the American *Elmore*, manufactured between 1900 and 1911, according to the *Saturday Evening Post*, and 1900 and 1912, according to D. C. Field. There are some successful manufacturers of two-stroke engines today but there were few when the Elmore Manufacturing Company of Clyde, Ohio, started in business. The Elmore Company made no other type of engine until their demise, although during those eleven or twelve years they progressed from single-cylinder to four. An Elmore, 1904 vintage, made its début in the 1972 Brighton Run.

More obscure is the story of the *Etna*, built by H. F. Harding, of the Brixton Motor Works in London. Described as a tandem tricycle, the 1904 Etna is generally reckoned to have been an experiment although later the firm made some four-wheeled cars. A tandem tricycle regularly takes part in the Brighton Run and there is documentary evidence of the existence of Etnas in 1905, 1906, 1908, 1914 and 1924. The car does not, however, appear in the *Saturday Evening Post* list and, so, presumably, never reached the shores of America.

*Eagle* was a popular car-name in the States but it appears that there were at least eight manufacturers using this name. It is perhaps just as well that none of them existed for more than three years. Had two or three of them proved successful, a number of lawsuits might have resulted.

Nor, alas, did everybody rush to buy *Everybody's*, a car which eked out an uncertain existence between 1908 and 1909 before finally expiring.

*Fifth Avenue Coach* is perhaps the most exotic-sounding car amongst the 'F' range but the 1912 production *Fwick* must surely present the most unusual spelling. *Ford* is of course the greatest name and it is difficult to find anything to say about this fantastic motoring success story which has not been said a million times before. Oddly enough, and despite their early history, Fords have only been rarely represented in the Brighton Run in contrast to another American automotive product, the *Franklin*. These were cars very much ahead of their time, so much so that Denis Field has declared that the popular Mini of today owes

## The Motor Car's Hall of Fame

something to the design of the early Franklin. Manufactured by the H. H. Franklin Manufacturing Company, of Syracuse, New York, the cars were air-cooled and the earliest models had a transverse four-cylinder engine, mounted ahead of the dash and with single chain drive to the rear axle.

In 1905, Franklin were advertising, 'Air-cooling doesn't cool, eh? How about that Franklin 15-day record from San Francisco to New York—4500 miles in August weather—600 miles through the Great American Desert. Could any other American automobile have done it?'

Mark you, record-breaking in those days had its snags. *The Automobile*, of February 6th, 1908, reporting another record run by a Franklin, 96 hours non-stop with the engine running all the time, even when the car was in a garage, said: 'During the course of Friday's run, Dailey (the Franklin driver) was unfortunate enough to encounter a farmer riding a horse. The latter became scared at the car and proceeded to bolt. The car was stopped and Dailey tried to pacify the farmer. The latter insisted on his stopping the engine, but as this would defeat his project, Dailey declined to accede. A constable arrested the entire party and took them to Lima, Maryland, where a magistrate fined Dailey 47 dollars and costs but the latter phoned the States' attorney. He advised the magistrate that he had exceeded his rights and that the highest fine he could assess was 5 dollars and costs.'

Despite such trials and tribulations, Franklin cars continued in production until 1934.

The Italians, with some justification, would challenge Ford as the greatest name in the 'F' category. And why not, when they can boast of F.I.A.T. (the full stops disappeared from the name in 1906), a name which dominated the headlines in the early days of motor racing and record breaking, a name which can be seen on hundreds of thousands of small cars today? Oddly enough, F.I.A.T. has been poorly represented in events like the Brighton Run.

The Italian flag was first carried in the Run in 1962 when Count L. Castelbarco Pindemonte, of Milan, winner in a *Maserati* of the 1934 Eifelrennen, brought across the Channel an 1899 *Menon*.

A Brighton regular is the *Gardner-Serpollet Steamer*. Gardner was an American with money, Serpollet an inventor with ideas. Serpollet built his first steam tricycle in 1887 and after Gardner had injected some money into the project, the manufacture of steam cars began around 1900, the first Gardner-Serpollet being seen in the States in 1901.

The *Georges Richard* also originated in France, beginning with a voiturette modelled largely on the Benz and going on to larger cars with vertical engines. The firm became known as *Richard-Brasier* and then simply as *Brasier*, this being the make which won the Gordon Bennett race for France in 1904 and again in 1905.

Another pioneer French firm was *Gladiator* which started before 1900 manufacturing cycles and voiturettes and went on first to light cars and then to heavier ones. The larger models were fitted with Aster engines and in 1909, certain Gladiator models were built by the *Austin* Motor Company at Longbridge, Birmingham.

Only one car is known to survive of another French make, *Gillet-Forest*, a steam car built in Paris by a Monsieur Gillet. A 1902 model holds Dating Certificate No. 1 of the Veteran Car Club and has frequently taken part in the Brighton Run.

Some rare 'Gs' originated in the States, amongst them not surprisingly a whole succession of 'Greats'—*Great Arrow, Great Eagle, Great Southern, Great Western, Great Smith* (great who?) and, simply, *Great*, most of which appear to have failed to live up to the nomenclature bestowed upon them by their proud designers. One manufacturer at least had a literary bent, the *Goethemobile* flitting briefly across the scene in 1902.

Although there were many cars marketed in the States with 'H' as the first letter of their name, there were comparatively few on the European side of the Atlantic. Of these, *Humber* may well be the most famous. The firm became known as cycle manufacturers as early as 1868 and around the turn of the century began producing cars. A novel feature of their 1901 models was a radiator which swung downwards so as to give access to the engine. The following year, Humber came up with another unique feature, a steering column adjustable for both height and rake. *Humberette* is from the same stable. In modern times, Humber were taken over by the Rootes Group which in turn was swallowed up by the American Chrysler empire.

Much more rare than the Humber is the *Hanzer*, made in Paris by the Hanzer Brothers from 1900 to 1902. Only one of the 1902 models is known to survive and it is powered by the ubiquitous Aster engine.

A well-known US make in the early days, product of the Hupp Motor Company, of Detroit, was the *Hupmobile*. First manufactured in 1908, by 1911 the makers were claiming that their car was 'the first touring car with sliding-gear transmission and Bosch magneto to be sold for less than one thousand dollars.'

'I' could be for *Imperial* which was one of the names under which single-cylinder cars built by the Paris firm of *Lacoste & Battman* were fitted with English-built bodies and marketed in the British Isles. During the period 1903 to 1905, these cars were sold under many different names and, apart from Imperial, the best-known are probably *Napoleon* and *Speedwell*.

Variations on 'International' were popular on both sides of the Atlantic—there were five in the United States alone. More familiar to British enthusiasts are the products of the International Motor Company, of London, which sold a variety of hybrids and originals, amongst them the *International Benz* which was either constructed from Benz components or had a Benz chassis with an English-built body. The *International Charette* of the same company was, however, an original, being built especially for them at Coventry. It was introduced in 1900 and an improved version came out the following year.

An ill-fated venture which, perhaps, deserved better fortune was that of W. H. McIntyre, of Auburn, Indiana, who in 1913 'introduced the Cyclecar to America'. Known as the *Imp*, it had a two-cylinder air-cooled engine, four wheels, and sold for only 375 dollars. But it didn't catch on and only a few were built. It was to be many years before another little Imp became established when the Rootes Group introduced the Hillman Imp to the modern world.

*Jack's Runabout* at least had the most delightful name of the

'Js' in American car history but in Britain there was the more illustrious *James & Browne*. These cars are now rare birds and only two, a 1902 version and a 1904, have made regular appearances in the Brighton Run. The former is owned by the City & Guilds College Motor Club and usually 'crewed' by students. The other is owned by S. E. Procter, whose father assisted in building the cars originally. James & Browne cars were built at Hammersmith, London, the first production model coming out of the factory in 1901. It embodied a horizontal engine, mounted amidships. Both two and four-cylinder models were made until 1906 when they were replaced by four and six-cylinder Vertex models.

One of the oldest cars leads the 'K' parade, the *Knight*, built in Britain in 1895. The designer and owner was fined for not having a traction engine licence and for not being preceded by a man on foot. The sentence was 2s. 6d. fine and 10s. 0d. costs on each charge.

The most famous American car in the 'Ks' was probably the *Knox*, which had many early racing successes to its credit. *King* was a common name but the best-established of these appears to have been the King Motor Car Company of Detroit who were in busines for at least seven years. Claiming to be the first to introduce a cantilever spring car to America, they marketed an eight-cylinder car, which, it was boasted, would out-perform all others.

Then, in our alphabetical progression, we come to one of the truly great names of automobilism—*Lanchester*. Dr. Lanchester, one of three brothers, designed and built the first four-wheeled petrol-engined car to be manufactured in Britain from British designs. This was constructed in Birmingham between the years 1895 to 1896. Bristling with ideas and unique features, the Lanchesters were to continue in production for many, many years. From the very beginning all models used a pre-selector gear-box and a very successful worm final drive was used at a time when many cars had open chains. George Lanchester, the youngest brother, lived on until quite recently, a charming and courteous gentleman, who was always

23. Designers of model cars work hard to be accurate these days. Fred Rix and Ken Whetton, of the Lesney 'Matchbox' series, check up on cars in the Measham Motor Museum, near Burton-on-Trent

24. The 1904 Vauxhall, with which the author appeared on television, alongside a modern Vauxhall Viva. In the background, Vauxhall's new engineering centre

25. Former world motor racing champion Graham Hill takes the wheel of a 1903 Wolseley in the 1972 London to Brighton Run. Wrapped up well in the back is actress Dora Bryan

26. Believed to be the third oldest petrol-driven vehicle in the world, the 1886 Hammel, took part in the 1954 Brighton Run. The inventor was a Danish blacksmith named Hans Urban Johansen, the car taking its name from his employer

27. Denis Flather, in his 1897 Daimler, drives the Lord Mayor of Nottingham to the opening of the RAC's 75th Anniversary Exhibition, *The Age of the Motor Car*, in that city

28. One of the great racing cars of the pioneer days, the Rolland-Pilain, seen at a re-union at Pau in 1957

29. The author makes a presentation to one of Britain's leading car designers, Donald Healey, after the latter had opened the RAC's 75th Anniversary Exhibition in Plymouth. Centre is Captain 'Bill' Gregson, of the RAC

30. C. Chester Smith, of the Pembrokeshire Motor Museum, drives the local MP to the opening of the RAC's 75th Anniversary Exhibition in a 1903 Oldsmobile. The venue was Tenby, South Wales

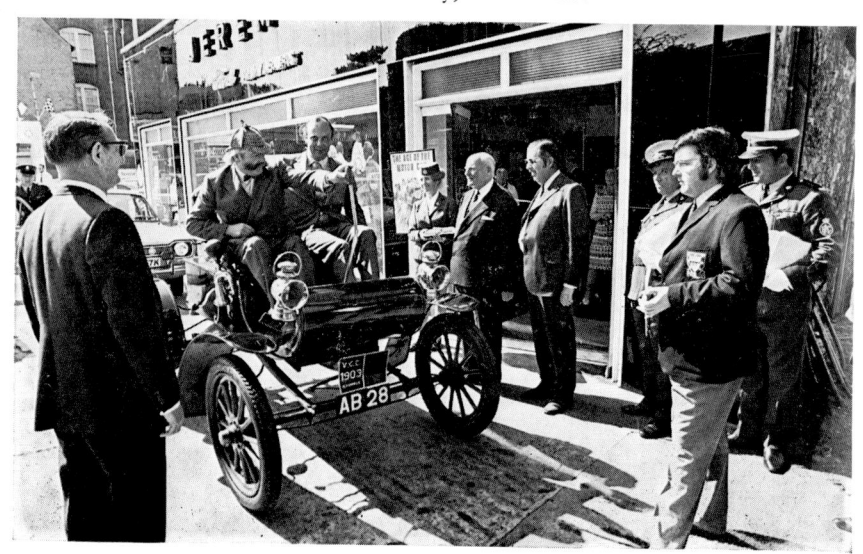

## The Motor Car's Hall of Fame

anxious to support veteran and vintage events and rarely missed the Brighton Run. One year when he did not have a ride, he was to be seen standing amongst the spectators at Hyde Park in the pouring rain, avoiding the VIP treatment which his place in the history of motoring had earned.

A great name in the early days of the French motor industry was *Léon Bollée*. First made at Le Mans in 1896, these three-wheelers were very popular at one time and perhaps surprisingly had many racing successes. References to these unusual cars is made elsewhere in these pages. An English version was also marketed, under the name *Coventry Motette*.

Another three-wheeler from France but much more obscure than the Bollée, is the *La Nef*. Manufactured by Lacroix & de Laville, they were powered by De Dion engines. These cars are accepted for the Brighton Run although reliable evidence as to their age is scarce.

From the States comes the *Locomobile Steamer*. The Stanley brothers built their first steam car in 1897 but in 1899, the business was sold to the Locomobile Company who then marketed the cars under their own name. Very lightly-built, the Steamers were nothing much more than a boiler mounted on four wheels with seats for two and in 1903, Locomobile changed over to petrol cars, continuing these until about 1929.

*Lutzmann* cars were made in Germany from 1895 onwards and the story of those imported to this country is told elsewhere. The *Opel* car of today is a descendant of the Lutzmann, although one would have to look very hard to see the slightest resemblance between the two.

Of the many United States 'Ls' the best-known apart from Locomobile is probably the *Lozier*, again a car which achieved racing success in the early days. But America preserves a cheeky air with *Lad's Car*, which was manufactured briefly in 1914.

Daimler founded the German Daimler Company after inventing his high-speed engine in 1885 and the early cars from the factory were known as Canstatt-Daimlers. This went on until 1901 when a revolutionary new design was evolved, so different from the early cars that it was decided it must have a completely different name. Thus came into being *Mercedes*, after the daughter of one of company's directors. The rest of the Mercedes story is writ large in the history books.

A famous pioneer Belgian firm was *Minerva*, which like many others, began with the manufacture of motor-cycles and motor-cycle engines. From France, Paris to be precise, came the *Mors*, cars which even in 1896 were ahead of their time and which won many motor-racing victories. The Mors had a V-type four-cylinder engine at a time when most manufacturers were content with one or two cylinders. Also from France but not nearly so well-known was the *M.L.B.*, made at Hondouville by the firm of Landry & Beyroux. These were built between 1894 and 1902, the earlier models being very heavy with large wooden-spoked wheels and a single-cylinder engine mounted at the rear. In 1901, a much lighter model with wire wheels was produced and one of these has taken part in the Brighton Run.

*MMC* stood for the Motor Manufacturing Company of Great Britain which developed from the Great Horseless Carriage Company of 1896. During a somewhat chequered career, the company produced a number of models fitted with Daimler engines and bearing other similarities, not surprising since they were built under the same roof in the Coventry factory.

Talking of similarities, the *Milwaukee Steamer* bore a close resemblance to the Locomobile. Built in Milwaukee, Wisconsin, they were on the market from 1900 to 1902 in the form of light steam cars and heavy steam commercial vehicles.

*Napier*, one of the earliest British manufacturers, have a proud record, successfully completing the great Thousand Miles Trial of 1900, setting records at Brooklands with S. F. Edge at the wheel, acquitting themselves well in the Tourist Trophy races and, perhaps above all, scoring Britain's first big international motor racing success when Edge took the Gordon Bennet Cup in 1902.

*New Orleans*, despite the name were manufactured at Twickenham, Middlesex, and the first models were based upon the Belgian *Vivinus* cars. Two of them took part in the Thousand Miles Trial.

## The Motor Car's Hall of Fame

And just to complete the geographical confusion, the *Norfolk* was made at Cleckheaton, Yorkshire, by the firm of A. Blackburn. Only one is believed to have survived.

A truly famous name, not only in America its country of origin but throughout the world, is *Oldsmobile*, now part of General Motors, and which celebrated its 75th Anniversary in 1972. The story started in fact back in 1895 when two young men from Lansing, Michigan, Ransom E. Olds and Frank Clark, decided to try to build a carriage driven by a gasoline engine, the elder Olds being a manufacturer of stationary engines and Clark's father owning a carriage works. After this first vehicle ran successfully, the Olds Motor Vehicle Company was formed with a capital of 50,000 dollars. Olds found Lansing too much of 'a small pond' however and in 1899 having secured the necessary financial backing, moved to Detroit where the Olds Motor Works was founded with a capital of 350,000 dollars. It was here that the famous Oldsmobile curved-dash runabout was developed and manufactured on a progressive assembly system, forerunner of today's mass production. The Detroit factory burned down in 1901 but Lansing offering a 52-acre site free, Olds moved back to his original base.

The curved-dash, examples of which frequently take part in the Brighton Run, hit the headlines in a big way and production soon soared to over 5,000 vehicles a year. Roy E. Chapin drove one from Detroit to New York over nearly impassable muddy roads and canal tow paths in seven and a half days, averaging 14 mph and using 30 gallons of gasoline. His feat made the car the hit of the 1902 New York Motor Show. The following year the Olds 'Pirate' established a world record of five miles in $6\frac{1}{2}$ minutes on the sands of Daytona Beach, Florida, and the same car covered the measured mile in less than one minute.

In 1905, there was a transcontinental race between two curved-dash models from New York City to Portland, Oregon. Dwight B. Huss, driving 'Old Scout', defeated Percy F. Megargel in 'Old Steady', covering the 4,000 miles in 44 days. Olds himself had by now left the company after internal disagreements but the Oldsmobile was now immortal, Gus Edwards having composed the song, 'In My Merry Oldsmobile', which was to sweep the States.

Another Brighton regular is the *Orient Express* which was manufactured no nearer China than Gaggenau, Germany. Made by a firm called Bergmann's between 1895 and 1903, they were sold in London from about 1898 onwards.

Far more obscure is the *Owen*, an American make not to be confused with the *Owen-Magnetic*. Built between 1910 and 1914, the former is worthy of mention since it represented an effort to produce a car capable of coping on long cross-country journeys with the poor roads of the time. The car had a powerful engine, enormous wheels, a high ground clearance and driver and passengers had to climb two steps to get in. Presumably, road improvements eventually made the Owen obsolete. The Owen-Magnetic was in production from 1915 until 1921 and there was also the *Owen-Schoeneck* (1915–16) and the *Owen Thomas* (1908). The punsters amongst American manufacturers had a great time with the 'Os', as witness, *Onlicar* and *O-We-Go*.

It is not generally realised that Czechoslovakia, or its constituent countries, has played a prominent role in the story of the automobile.

Steam vehicles were first built in Bohemia by Joseph Bozek, the first public demonstration being given in Prague on Sunday, September 24th, 1815. It was highly successful and is claimed to be the first drive of a steam car on the European continent after the memorable experiments of Cugnot. Nothing much happened, however, until 1886 when Ludvik Baffrey built a steam car, which included some new developments. Then came an electric car, designed in 1895 by Frantisek Krizik.

These efforts with steam and electricity paled into insignificance with the inventions of Benz and Daimler and the Czech motor industry began the manufacture of *President* cars at Koprivnice in Moravia. The Presidents were built according to Benz's original drawings but the Czechs soon produced designs of their own. In later years, this same factory was to become the headquarters of the *Tatra* concern and their director Jan Ledwinka is reckoned to be one of the great designers in automative

## The Motor Car's Hall of Fame

history, his small cars having influenced the development of European automobile design.

There were other irons in the Czech fire. *Laurin and Klement*, with a factory at Mlada Boleslav, began car manufacture in 1905 and soon became a force to be reckoned with, exporting to Japan and Turkestan amongst other countries. L & K enjoyed many racing successes too, particularly when Otto Hieronymus was in their employ. Other companies followed including *Praga*, *Walter* and *Velox*. In the post-war period, some of these Czech cars, notably Laurin-Klement, have come across to Britain for veteran car events.

The President has led us astray, alphabetically speaking, so back to a very famous name, *Packard*. The first Packard car was built by two brothers of that name in 1899 at Warren, Ohio. It had a single-cylinder, horizontal engine, tiller steering and wire wheels. In 1901, wheel steering was introduced and the Packard concern went on to become one of the great names in the United States automobile industry. Luxury and comfort were always Packard bywords and as early as 1912, the company was advertising 'electric self-starter; electric lighting; starting, ignition, lighting and carburetor controls on steering column.' Such refinements did not come cheap and Packards of the time cost between 4,150 and 5,400 dollars.

*Peerless* was another great name in the United States. The company began in 1869 making bicycles and later, of all things, clothes wringers. The Peerless 'horseless carriage' made its bow in 1900, powered with a De Dion engine. Then a designer named Louis Mooers joined the company and real progress was made. The company concentrated on high-quality but moved into motor sport when Barney Oldfield, who had made his name on the tracks driving for Ford, joined Peerless to drive the 'Green Dragon'. Oldfield's fantastic string of successes in this car boosted Peerless sales considerably but the financial ups and downs of the late twenties and early thirties saw the demise of the car. And, believe it or not, after ceasing automobile production, the company reorganised itself as the Brewing Corporation of America and began bottling Carling beer.

Another American car of the early days was the *Pope-Tribune*, only one example of which is known to exist in England with another in Eire. This car was built between 1904 and 1906 but there are a number of other cars incorporating Pope in their names, amongst them *Pope-Hartford* (1895–1912), *Pope Motor* (1903), *Pope Robinson* (1902–4), *Pope-Toledo* (1903–9), *Pope Waverley Electric* (1903–7) and simply, *Pope* (1903).

Undeterred by the high casualty rate amongst automobile manufacturers, the humorists still abounded and we had at this time the *Poppy Car*, the *Powercar*, the *Preferred*, the *Premocar*, and the *Pridemore*.

In Europe, some very famous names come under the heading 'P'. First of all comes *Panhard et Levassor*, the famous French firm which began car production many years before it became legal to drive a car in Great Britain without being preceded by a man on foot. The part this company played in the growth of the car industry cannot be described in a few lines but it is probably true to say that, more than any other firm, the French factory turned the inventions of Benz and Daimler into practical channels, so much so that even today the majority of cars still follow the general layout of the early Panhards. As with so many of the pioneer companies, racing played its part in making Panhard-Levassor famous.

Another great French name is that of *Peugeot*. The first of their vehicles was built in 1890 by Armand Peugeot at Beaulieu, France, and by 1897 demand was such that the firm opened two new factories.

Charles Rolls introduced the Peugeot to Britain in 1895. Until 1896, Peugeots used a rear-mounted Daimler engine but after this, engines of their own design were employed.

Also from France came *Phebus-Aster*, voiturettes fitted with one-cylinder engines at the rear. These cars were sold in England as *Automobilettes*.

From Belgium came the *Pieper*, a car with a very mixed ancestry. The first models were very similar to the English New Orleans which was itself of Belgian parentage. They were fitted with De Dion engines.

*Pick* cars, although largely forgotten now, had a comparatively long life. Manufactured at Stamford, the range began at the turn of the century with a four-wheeled Sociable with its

## The Motor Car's Hall of Fame

engine at the rear. Voiturettes and light cars followed and the firm continued in production as late as 1925.

The *Phoenix* car owes its being to one of the pioneers of motoring and motor-cycling in Britain, Van Hooydonk. He evolved the *Phoenix Motor-cycle* to which a chair could be fitted in place of the normal front wheel for which was substituted two wheels and an axle.

This gave way to a design in which the chair, or forecar, was a permanent fixture and this model was known as the *Phoenix Trimo*. This was followed by the *Phoenix Quad* car and then, in 1907, by the Phoenix light car.

There are not many 'Q' cars in the lists. The United States had the *Queen* (1902–6), the *Quick* (1899–1900) and the *Quinlin* (1904). Britain had the *Quadrant*. One of the earliest firms in the cycle trade, the Quadrant Cycle Co. Ltd., of Birmingham, started production of motor-cycles and tricycles early in the present century and then went on to cars. One of their more ingenious designs was a three-wheeler made in 1903 which incorporated two entirely independent engines. Their 1902 tricycle had an equally ingenious steering arrangement whereby the machine leaned inwards on corners in the same way as a bicycle.

'R' stands for *Renault*, another of the great pioneering names France has given to the automobile industry. The firm was founded by three brothers, Marcel, Louis and Fernand, their early cars being fitted with De Dion engines. Later they developed the design in which the radiator was placed between the engine and the dashboard, the airtight bonnet with its distinctive shape being retained for many years, even after the radiator was moved back to the conventional position.

The Renault brothers themselves had a tragic history. Marcel was killed in the notorious Paris–Madrid race of 1903, the 'Race of Death'; Fernand was killed during the Second World War when a bomb fell on his house in Paris; and Louis, in the accusations and counter-accusations of collaboration which wracked France after the war, was first imprisoned then beaten to death as he lay in hospital.

There were outstanding 'R' names in Britain too. *Rover*, for example. The Rover Cycle Company began the manufacture of cycles in Coventry in 1877, added motor-cycles to the catalogue at the beginning of the century and in 1903 produced a forecar. The *Rover Motor Tandem* appeared in 1904 followed almost immediately by the first true Rover car. This was an 8 horse-power, single-cylinder model which had no chassis in the normal sense but a cast aluminium box girder which ran from engine to rear axle.

Rovers later established a reputation for building solid cars in the near-luxury class but this enterprising firm, still in production today as part of the giant British Leyland complex, has also been responsible for that most versatile of utility vehicles, the *Land Rover*, and also for the development of jet turbine cars. I once had the privilege of driving in the first of these cars, JET 1, a remarkable and never-to-be-forgotten experience.

Equally-famed is the *Riley*. The first experimental Riley car was made in 1898, after which the Riley Cycle Company made motor-cycles, tricycles and quadricycles, the two last being based upon De Dion Bouton models and sold under the name of *Royal Riley*. In 1902, the first tricar of Riley's own design was built and in 1906, the first four-wheeled V-twin 9 horsepower Riley car was produced.

Later the company was to enjoy tremendous prestige in sporting and racing circles and especially remembered are the Riley TT achievements of the twenties and thirties in the hands of drivers like Gillow, Freddie Dixon, McClure and Whitcroft. Rileys, unfortunately ended as badge and radiator cars in the British Leyland empire.

Also from Coventry came the *Rex* Motor Manufacturing Company which was making motor-cycles and cars as early as 1902. They had a penchant for tricycles and tricars. The earlier type, known as the *Rex Triette*, and later model, the *Rexette*, were not perhaps happily named, rude people suggesting that the names had double meanings.

The Enfield Cycle Company was yet another firm of bicycle manufacturers who took to motor tricycles and quadricycles. This sort of production started at Redditch in 1899 and within a few years the company was making *Royal Enfield* voiturettes and

## The Motor Car's Hall of Fame

light cars. In the sequel, however, car production was discontinued and Royal Enfield continued for many years as a famous name in the world of cycles and motor-cycles.

*Scania* cars are of Swedish origin and were built at Malmö from 1902 to 1911 in which year the firm amalgamated with another Swedish firm, *Vabis*. Today, Scania are better-known for lorries, the car side being taken care of by the rally-winning *Saab*.

The earliest genuine *Siddeley* car was made by the Wolseley Company at Crayford, Kent, in 1904–5. From 1906 to 1910, the cars were known as *Wolseley-Siddeleys* and later the name was associated with Deasy in the *Siddeley-Deasy* car.

The *Star* comes from yet another cycle company, the Star Company of Wolverhampton, who began making cars in the nineties. Early models bore a strong resemblance to the Benz and are sometimes referred to as *Star-Benz*. A 1904 model, 'Twinkle', in splendid condition and owned by Peter Newens, of Kew, takes part regularly in the Brighton Run and has twice been chosen by the Royal Automobile Club for display in the Club's entrance hall, the second occasion being upon the visit of Her Majesty the Queen, to commemorate the Club's 75th Anniversary in 1972.

Earlier we mentioned the Stanley brothers of USA who built steam cars in 1897 then sold out to Locomobile. In 1901, the Stanley brothers started again on their own account and had obviously learned much in the intervening period since the *Stanley Steamer* was so successful that it continued in production until 1927.

One of the oldest British veteran cars, of which only one model survives, is the 1898 *Stephens*. Built by a firm of cycle and general engineers in Clevedon, Somerset, the Stephens has been a Brighton Run regular for many years and was for a long time owned and driven by a grandson of the original designer. He (the grandson) was at one time President of the Veteran Car Club.

The first *Sunbeam* car is claimed to have been built in 1899 but no model was marketed until 1901. Four-cylinder models were made from 1902, the first of these being based upon the successful French *Berliet* car. An early product was the 1901

*Sunbeam Mabley* which is a Brighton regular. The subsequent Sunbeam history with its links with Talbot and Darracq and so on is a complicated one but the name is best remembered because of the exploits of Sir Henry Segrave, both on the race circuits where he won the French and Spanish Grand Prix, and in the realm of the world land speed record.

*Swift* of Coventry were another cycle firm who subsequently made a great success of car production. The first Swift motor car was made in 1901 and later many awards were won by the Swift single- and twin-cylinder voiturettes. The car remained one of the most popular on the English roads until the firm went into liquidation during the slump of 1931.

The Swift did not deserve to die; the American firm which dared to produce a car called *Silent Knight* surely did.

An American Bicycle Company, called, aptly enough, just that, produced the *Toledo Steamer*. Like all the American steam cars of the period, it was based very closely upon the Stanley-Locomobile vehicles.

Another steamer, the *Turner-Miesse* began life as a Belgian product under the name *Miesse* but in 1902, Turner's Motor Manufacturing Company Ltd., of Wolverhampton, began to build them under licence and by 1904, the vehicle was being sold as the Turner-Miesse. It was a simple design compared with other steam cars of the period and continued in production until 1913. By this time, the *Turner* petrol car had become established and these continued until 1929.

*Thornycroft* today means heavy commercial vehicles and marine engines but the firm did make cars between 1903 and 1913. Early models were 10 and 20 horsepower and later a 45 hp six-cylinder car was marketed. Several examples still exist and two of them frequently take part in the Brighton Run.

Only two *Tony Huber* cars are known to exist. This was a French firm which built both engines and complete cars in the early years of the century.

'U' seems to be a rare initial amongst European and British manufacturers, *Unic* being the only one coming readily to mind but in the States, the situation has been different. Apart from a

## The Motor Car's Hall of Fame

car called the *Ulster* which appeared in 1939, there were fourteen manufacturers whose products, if any still survive, would now be labelled as veterans—*Ultimate*, two versions of *Union, United, United Motor, Unito, Universal, University, Unwin, Upton, U.S., U.S. Electric, U.S. Long Distance,* and *U.S. Motor Vehicle.* Most of these had very brief lives and would appear to qualify for the more modern usage of US.

The 'Vs' too were generally short-lived but on this side of the Atlantic, a proud name still in business is that of *Vauxhall.* The Vauxhall Iron Works started in business in 1857, primarily as manufacturers of steam engines. Car production began in 1903 and a 1904 model has been a Brighton Run regular. The genius of designer Laurence Pomeroy the elder brought later Vauxhalls to the forefront and the make has long been a well-established favourite in Britain although today Vauxhall are the British division of the giant General Motors organisation.

*Vulcan* built their first production cars in 1902 although it was claimed that their first experimental car saw the light of day in 1899. Vulcans were marketed in the States between 1913 and 1915.

The *Whitney Steamer* hailed from Boston, Mass., where George E. Whitney built his first steam car in 1896. By 1899, the Whitney was being built under licence by the Stanley brothers who had sold their own patents to Locomobile. The vehicles were imported and sold in the UK by Brown Brothers, who described them as *Brown-Whitney.* One of these cars took part in the Thousand Miles Trial of 1900.

Another steamer of American origin was the *White.* From 1903 onwards, all White models had compound steam engines under the bonnet in front with a condenser mounted where the normal radiator would be, thus being similar in appearance to an ordinary petrol car.

*Winton* was another well-known American make, the first model making its appearance in 1897. They continued in production until 1924 and chalked up a great many competition successes.

In 1895, the first *Wolseley*, a three-wheeler was designed by

## The Book of the Veteran Car

Herbert Austin (later Lord Austin) who was responsible for the design of all Wolseley models until he left to found the Austin Motor Company in 1905. As mentioned earlier, the cars were known as Wolseley-Siddeley from 1906 to 1910, then reverted simply to Wolseley. In their final years, these cars were to become another one of the 'badge and radiator' marques in the British Leyland combine.

One could go on seemingly for ever with notes on the thousands of makes which have peppered the comparatively short history of the automobile but it may be fitting to end with the *Wartburg*, which carries the East German banner in automotive competition today and has done surprisingly well in events such as the RAC International Rally of Great Britain. The Wartburg story began with one Heinrich Ehrhardt who built and marketed his first cars in 1898 under the name of *Eisenach*. Most of these were electric-powered although one model had a rear-mounted Benz engine. Very soon, Ehrhardt discontinued his own designs and reached agreement with Decauville, the French manufacturers, to build their cars under licence. These were sold as Wartburgs, a name taken from the castle looming above the town of Eisenach.

There are many more makes of car than those listed here and many more stories to be unearthed about them by the keen motoring historian. That is one of the great pleasures of making veteran cars your hobby. For myself, I must express thanks for much of the information in this chapter to Dennis C. Field, historian of the Veteran Car Club; the pages of *Autocar*, *Motor*, the *Veteran and Vintage Magazine* and the *Saturday Evening Post*; and to that late lamented good friend, the American collector and historian, Floyd Clymer.

Many were the blithe spirits who set off to seek fame and fortune as automobile manufacturers, few were those who successfully survived.

Yet all of those mentioned here and many others must have secretly been imbued by the same enthusiasm as prompted one to advertise: 'I am Russell E. Gardner, the "Buggy King" of St. Louis, USA. BANNER BUGGIES BEAT THE WORLD.'

Well, perhaps they didn't—but at least they had a darn good try.

# Index

Achilles, 116
Acme, 37
AEC, 65, 101
Albany, 80, 81
Albert, 94
Albion, 44, 65, 101, 116
Alfa-Romeo, 65
Allchin, 82
Alldays, 116
Alvis, 69
American Power Carriage, 116
American Voiturette, 116
Anglo-French Phaeton, 25
Apperson, 115
Arden, 69
Ariel, 30, 31, 35, 65
Arielette, 70
Argyll, 100, 116
Armstrong-Siddeley, 69
Arnold Motor Carriage, 19, 21, 25, 42, 45, 46, 116
Arrol-Aster, 70
Arrol-Johnston, 70, 117
Aster (Whitlock-, West-), 117, 119
Auburn, 48, 53, 116
Austin, 64, 99, 126, 140
Auto-Bug, 117
Autocar, 117
Auto Fore Carriage, 116
Automobile Forecarriage, 116
Automobile Voiturette, 116
Automote, 116

Badger, 115
Baker Electric/Steam, 117
Banner Boy Buckboard, 81
Banner Buggies, 140
Barker, 52, 83
Bat, 65
Beau Chamberlain, 115
Beaufort, 98, 118
Beeston, 23
Belsize, 53
Ben-Hur, 115
Bentley, 52, 65, 82, 83, 84, 99
Benz (International-), 35, 41, 42, 46, 47, 48, 49, 50, 54, 73, 82, 89, 90, 102, 107, 111, 112, 116, 118, 127, 140
Berliet, 137
Bersey, 25, 67
Black Crow, 115
'Blue Bird', 65
Blumberg, 115
Bollée, Leon, 18, 19, 21, 22, 25, 41, 43, 44, 50, 51, 110, 129
Bremer, 47
Briscoe, 76
Britannia Electric, 25
Browne, Samuel, 73
Brush, 118
Brushmobile, 118
Buffalo Electric, 119
Bugatti, 65, 72, 74, 82
Buick, 90, 115

Cadillac, 42, 44, 75, 78, 82, 90, 106, 113, 115, 118, 119
Canstatt-Daimler, 19, 64, 66, 129
Carane-Simplex, 76
Carter Twin-Engine, 120
Celer, 119
Century (Tandem), 43, 119
C.G.V., 119
Champion Electric, 120
Charron, 102, 119
Chatham, 120
Chelsea, 120
Chevrolet, 89
Chicago, 120
Chrysler, 64, 115
Citroën, 64, 89
Clement-Panhard (Stirling-Panhard), (Clement-Talbot) (Talbot), (Clement-Bayard) (Bayard), 120
Commer, 101
Contal, 36
Corre, 120
Coventry-Climax (Simplex), 68, 69
Coventry-Humber, 98
Creanche, 120
Crosley, 115

141

## Index

Crossley, 101
Crowden, Chas. T., 42
Csonka, 90
Cudell, 120
Cugnot, 71, 72, 89, 132

Dailey, 125
Daimler, 25, 28, 35, 42, 46, 50, 53, 59, 64, 67, 73, 78, 89, 90, 98, 118, 121
Darracq, 45, 49, 79, 84, 94, 95, 102, 121
Darracq-Bollée, 67
Decauville, 122
Dechamps, 123
DeDietrich, 84, 122
De Dion Bouton (Comte De Dion, M. Bouton), 22, 23, 24, 30, 34, 36, 41, 42, 44, 46, 49, 51, 52, 64, 71, 78, 90, 109, 120, 121, 134
Delage, 78
Delahaye, 47, 77, 90, 122
Delin, 122
Dennis, 99, 101, 122
De Soto, 115
Detroit Electric, 76
Dodge, 115
Dudgeon, 75
Duesenberg, 53
Dufaux, 74
Du Pont, 53
Durkopp (Cannello) (Watsonia), 122
Duryea, 19, 24, 25, 122

Eagle, 124
Eisenach, 140
Elmore, 124
English Mechanic, 123
ERA, 65, 93
Essex, 53
Etna, 124
Everybodys', 124
Excalibur, 81

Fiat, 48, 80, 83, 89, 102, 125
Fifth Avenue Coach, 124
F. N. Herstal, 90
Foden, 101
Fondu, 79
Ford, 54, 65, 76, 80, 89, 115, 124, 133
Ford Model T, 37, 38, 64, 78, 82, 83, 84, 85
Foster, 67
Fowler, 82

Franklin, 76, 124
Frazier, 115
Fwick, 124

Gabriel, 102
Galloway, 70
Gardner-Serpollet, 67, 126
Georges Richard, (Richard-Brasier) (Richard), 46, 102, 126
Gillet-Forest, 126
Gladiator, 126
Gobron-Brillie, 65
Goddard, 36
Goethemobile, 126
'Golden Arrow', 65
'Golden Eagle', 115
Gorton, 23
GRD, 71
Great, 126
Great Arrow, 126
Great Smith, 126
Great Southern, 126
Great Western, 126
Gregoire, 72
Guzzardi, 37
GWK, 69

Hammel, 44, 45
Hanzer, 127
Haynes-Apperson, 75
Haynes (Elwood), 123
Healey, 64
Hillman, 69, 99, 127
Hispano-Suiza, 65
Holsman, 75
Honda, 65
Horstmann, 99
Hudson, 115
Humber (Humberette), 43, 64, 99, 126, 127
Hupmobile, 127

Imp, 127
Imperial (Lacoste & Battman) (Napoleon) (Speedwell), 127
International Charette, 127
Invicta, 99
Iris, 99
Isotta-Fraschini, 102
Itala, 36, 37, 71, 83

Jack's Roundabout, 127
Jaguar, 69, 80
James & Browne, 100, 128
Jeanperrin, 49
Jowett, 101

142

## Index

King, 128
Knight, 64, 67, 128
Knox, 47, 48, 128

Lacroix-Delaville, 78
Lad's Car, 129
Lagonda, 43, 82, 99
'La Jamais Contente', 72
Lambert, 123
Lanchester, 31, 33, 34, 46, 67, 69, 84, 128
La Nef, 48, 129
Laurin & Klement, 48, 133
Lawson Steamer ('Craigievar Express'), 49, 108
Leader, 119
Leyland, 82, 101
Liberty, 92
Lincoln, 115
Locomobile Steamer, 30, 46, 48, 129, 137, 138
London Motor Van & Wagon Co., 31
Lotus, 65, 69
Lozier, 75, 129
Lutzmann, 50, 51, 100, 108, 110, 129

March-Ford, 65
Marcus, 72, 118
Marklin, 83
Marshall, 32, 33
Maserati, 125
Maudslay, 69
Maxwell, 65, 82, 84
McClure, 136
Mercedes (Benz), 42, 43, 48, 65, 73, 75, 82, 84, 90, 102, 111, 118, 130
Mercer, 84
Menon, 125
Mercury, 115
Merkel, 19
Milwaukee Steamer, 130
Minerva, 79, 130
Minoia, 102
MLB (Landry & Beyroux), 130
MMC, 30, 31, 35, 130
Mobile Steamer, 48
Morgan, 99
Morris, 64, 80, 82, 84, 99
Mors, 102, 130
Motor Carriage Supply Co., 31

Napier, 30, 33, 73, 75, 98, 130
Nash, 115
New Orleans, 130, 134
Norfolk, 131

Oldsmobile, 41, 43, 49, 50, 70, 81, 84, 115, 131
Onlicar, 132
Opel, 80, 82, 129
Orient Express, 30, 132
O-We-Go, 132
Owen, 132
Owen-Magnetic, 132
Owen-Schoeneck, 132
Owen-Thomas, 132

Packard, 75, 76, 82, 84, 115, 133
Panhard et Levassor (Panhard Daimler), 19, 20, 22, 25, 35, 40, 41, 45, 47, 48, 52, 67, 72, 89, 92, 101, 102, 119, 122, 133, 134
Panther, 80, 81
Payne & Bates, 69
Peerless, 133
Pennington, 24, 69
Peugeot, 34, 43, 48, 72, 82, 89, 93, 134
Phebus-Aster (Autimobillette), 134
Phoenix (Motor-cycle) (Trimo), (Quad), 135
Pick, 134
Pieper, 134
Pierce, 76
Plymouth, 53, 115
Pontiac, 115
Pope, 133
Pope-Hartford, 133
Pope Motor, 133
Pope-Robinson, 133
Pope-Toledo, 133
Pope-Tribune, 133
Pope Waverley, 133
Poppy Car, 133
Porsche, 65
Powercar, 133
Praga, 133
Preferred, 133
Premocar, 133
President, 90, 132
Pridemore, 133

Quadrant, 135
Queen, 135
Quick, 135
Quinlin, 135

Railton-Mobil, 69
Red Bug, 115
Red Wing, 115
Regal, 84
Reliant Scimitar, 64
Renault, 41, 53, 64, 75, 89, 102, 120, 135

143

## Index

Reo, 45, 48
Rex (Motor-cycle) (Triette) (Rexette), 65, 136
Rickenbacker, 76
Riley (Royal), 49, 69, 99, 136
Rio, 83
Rochet Schneider, 47, 89
Roger-Benz, 45, 67
Rolls-Royce, 44, 52, 53, 64, 67, 75, 78, 83, 84, 89, 98, 99, 100
Roots & Venables, 32
Roper, 75
Rover (Land Rover), 53, 69, 98, 99, 136
Royal Enfield, 136, 137
Rudge-Whitworth, 65

Saab, 137
Scania, 137
Sentinel, 101
Serpollet, 102
Shawmut, 37
Siddeley (-Deasy), 42, 69, 98, 99, 137
Silent Knight, 138
Simms Motor Wheel, 31, 33
Simplex, 76
Singer, 69
Spyker, 36, 73, 94, 95, 96
SS Motor Company, 32
Standard, 53, 68, 98
Stanley Steamer, 46, 64, 137, 138
Star (-Benz), 41, 137
Stephens, 41, 98, 137
Stoneleigh, 69
Studebaker, 115
Stutz, 82, 84
Sunbeam (-Mabley), 48, 53, 64, 65, 99, 101, 137, 138
Surrey, 80, 81
Swift, 67, 99, 138

Tatra, 132
Thames, 101
Thomas Flyer, 37, 82
Thorneycroft, 29, 41, 107, 138
Tilling-Stevens, 101
Toledo Steamer, 138
Tony Huber, 138

Triumph, 65, 69
Trojan, 64
Turner-Miesse, 138

Ulster, 139
Ultimate, 139
Unic, 138
Union, 139
Unipart, 50
United, 139
United Motor, 139
Unito, 139
Universal, 139
University, 139
Unwin, 139
Upton, 139
U.S. Electric, 139
U.S. Long Distance, 139
U.S. Motor Vehicle, 139

Vabis, 137
Vallee, 46
Vanden Plas, 53
Van Dyke, 115
Van Toll (Burford), 19, 31
Vanwall, 64
Vauxhall, 44, 64, 118, 139
Velox, 133
Viper, 41
Vivinus, 79, 130
Voigt, 119
Volkswagen, 64
Vulcan, 139

Wade, 89
Walter, 133
Wartburg, 140
White Steamer, 139
Whitney Steamer (Brown-Whitney) (George E), 139
Wiking, 89
Willys-Overland, 115
Winton, 139
Wolseley, 35, 36, 43, 47, 64, 67, 99, 137, 139

Zimmerman, 115